LIBRARY INSTRUCTION IN THE SEVENTIES: STATE OF THE ART

LIBRARY ORIENTATION SERIES

LIBRARY INSTRUCTION IN THE SEVENTIES:
STATE OF THE ART

Papers Presented at the Sixth Annual Conference
on Library Orientation for Academic Libraries
held at Eastern Michigan University, May 13-14, 1976

edited by
Hannelore B. Rader

Coordinator of the Education/Psychology Division
Center of Educational Resources
Eastern Michigan University

Published for the
Center of Educational Resources,
Eastern Michigan University
by

Pierian Press
ANN ARBOR, MICHIGAN
1977

Library of Congress Catalog Card No. 77-75678
ISBN 0-87650-078-5

PIERIAN PRESS
P.O. Box 1808
Ann Arbor, Michigan 48106

Contents

Preface

The Sixth Annual Conference on Library Orientation for Academic Libraries was held May 13 and 14, 1976 at Eastern Michigan University. This year we again exceeded our limit of one hundred participants by far and, unfortunately, we also had to turn a number of interested people away because of space limitations.

The Conference concentrated on the "state of the art of library instruction in the 70's," including state-of-the-art reports from Canada and the Middle East. Other reports focused on course-related library instruction and programmed library instruction using a workbook.

A panel discussion on evaluation of library instruction is available in recorded format. The audiocassette may be purchased from ACRL in Chicago.

Small discussion groups focused on "steps to follow to set up a program" and "how to implement a program." Guidelines which were used for these discussions are appended.

As in previous years, Ebsco Subscription Service hosted a cocktail party for all participants. This most enjoyable occasion let participants discuss library instruction issues in an informal setting.

This year we were most fortunate to have President James H. Brickley of Eastern Michigan University present the welcoming address to the Conference participants. His timely remarks on the problems in higher education in the 70's were very much appreciated.

We were also grateful to have Dr. Beverly Lynch, Executive Secretary of the Association of College and Research Libraries (ACRL) at the Conference. Her statement on ACRL's role in the 70's and how it relates to library instruction was most appropriate.

A note of appreciation must also be given to the following persons who, in addition to the speakers, served as discussion leaders and who, according to participants' evaluative comments, performed most admirably in this capacity: Anne Beaubien (University of

Michigan), Ronald Gardner (Adrian College), Mary George (University of Michigan), Rita Lichtenberg (Indiana University), Sharon Hogan (University of Michigan), Pamela Reeves (Eastern Michigan University), Anne Roberts (State University of New York at Albany), and Carla Stoffle (University of Wisconsin, Parkside).

The success of this year's Conference is due in large part to the extraordinary presentations of all speakers and the outstanding supportive services of the staff from EMU's conference services and the Center of Educational Resources. Special recognition for their services in making the Conference a success should go to Carolyn Kirkendall, Judy Sturgis Hill, Patricia McCreery, and Diane Posegay of the library staff.

Hannelore B. Rader
September 15, 1976

Introduction

I'm glad to see such a large attendance at the Sixth Annual Conference on Library Orientation for Academic Libraries. You may be interested to know that we have 147 librarians from 35 states and Canada in the audience - 118 institutions are represented.

This conference is in large part the result of the efforts of Hannelore Rader, our Orientation Librarian and Conference Coordinator. As some of you already know, her accomplishments in the field of library orientation have been recognized again by the Council on Library Resources, this time with a grant to identify and study ten successful library orientation programs and to write a guide for starting such programs. Carolyn Kirkendall, Director of Project LOEX, also played a major role in planning this Conference.

This year's theme is "Library Instruction in the 70's; A State of the Art." Now you have all heard the cliche that "Past is Prologue." Therefore, let me say a word about our past library orientation conferences as a prelude to the speakers who will follow.

EMU's Library Orientation Program was given great impetus by a joint National Endowment for the Humanities and Council on Library Resources Five-Year Grant covering the academic years 1970/71 through 1974/75. As an outgrowth of our own Library Orientation Program, the annual conferences were begun in May 1971.

The several conferences reflect changing trends. In the early stages, "Outreach" played a major role in the concept of library orientation - "Outreach" to non-users of libraries on campus, "Outreach to minorities, "Outreach" to veterans and other special groups, and "Outreach" to the lowly freshman. "Orientation" in these earlier days tended to be somewhat informal and unstructured.

Today the trend is towards more structured and formal programs, even including credit courses in library use offered by libraries and taught by librarians. I like to think – perhaps too optimistically -- that we've now "reached" our clientele and we're more concerned with the substantive content we make available to them. Thus, the term "Library Instruction" has generally replaced the earlier term "Library Orientation." It should be understood that I am using "Library Orientation" in the broadest sense to *include* "Library Instruction."

Each of the annual conferences focused on a different theme:

The first conference summarized the major issues as they appear-- ed in 1971, beginning with Millicent Palmer asking "Why Academic Library Instruction?"

The second, *A Challenge for Academic Libraries*, stressed how to *motivate* students to use the library.

The third dealt with *Planning and Developing a Library Orienta- tion Program*.

The fourth focused on the *objectives* of academic library in- struction.

The fifth stressed *faculty involvement* in library instruction.

The proceedings of the first five conferences are available from Pierian Press in Ann Arbor.

One of the panel presentations from the Fifth Conference, on the subject of "Faculty Views on Library Instruction," is also available on color video cassettes from the ALA Headquarters Li- brary in Chicago (standard interlibrary loan forms should be used.)

Now that library orientation programs have come of age, it is time to do a state--of--the--art review. Library orientation programs are an integral part of library service on an increasing number of campuses. The importance to the student of learning library--use skills cannot be over--estimated. Perhaps more than any other skills, these are a *must* for success in college, in graduate school and, most importantly, if I may quote from a speaker at our last conference, "for success in the process of self--education, a process that will continue long after our students leave our campus."

At his luncheon talk today, Dean A.P. Marshall will mention some of the library instruction programs which he has visited.

Sheila Laidlaw from the University of Toronto and Richard Dewey from the American University in Cairo will describe some programs in other countries.

One of the first library school courses specifically devoted to teaching librarians how to "instruct the library user" is being team-- taught by Mary George, Sharon Hogan, and Anne Beaubien at the University of Michigan. These three participated in a panel at our last conference. Fifteen of their students are in our audience today.

What is state--of--the--art thinking on some of the crucial issues in library instruction? For example, how do you plan and implement library orientation and instruction programs? The discussion groups today and tomorrow afternoons should generate some ideas.

Should the program be course–related and, if so, how? Tom Kirk of Earlham College will describe "course–related library instruction in the 70's."

What about credit courses and workbooks? Mimi Dudley from UCLA will present a review of this topic tomorrow morning.

How can you keep abreast of developments after you leave here? Carolyn Kirkendall will describe Project LOEX, a national clearing–house for information about library orientation and instruction programs. Be sure to see the LOEX exhibit and scan the LOEX newsletters.

Finally, when all is said and done, does your program work? Can such programs be evaluated and, if so, how? "Problems with Evalu–ating Library Instruction" will be the topic of a grand finale tomor–row afternoon in which you will hear again from some of the speak–ers who have appeared in this and earlier conferences. I believe this will be the most important discussion of this topic since a conference on the same subject was held at the University of Denver in 1973.

All in all, I wish you an interesting and enjoyable two days at Eastern Michigan University and hope you will take new ideas and memories of good fellowship with you when you leave.

Fred Blum
Director, Center of Educational Resources
Eastern Michigan University

LIBRARY INSTRUCTION IN THE 70's:
THE STATE OF THE ART IN CANADIAN
ACADEMIC LIBRARIES

Sheila M. Laidlaw
Sigmund Samuel Librarian
University of Toronto, Ontario

I'd like to thank Hannelore for her kind invitation to this year's Conference. I've enjoyed previous Conferences from the audience so I hope I may be able to contribute something from this end of the room -- but if you can't hear me, or don't understand something, or if you just want to ask a question, please raise your hand or shout and holler! I will also try to leave time at the end for questions and discussion.

I must admit my first reaction to the topic was to sum it up in one sentence: "You name it, we are doing it somewhere!" but immediately realized that that really wouldn't fill an hour or tell you much about the Canadian scene! As a first step I began to list what I saw as the major trends -- and now I've just heard Dr. Brickley summarize most of these same trends in relation to U.S. libraries! I felt that in recent years we had been giving less emphasis to individualized special instruction than in previous years.

My second major impression was that teaching excellence is becoming a real factor in the instruction process both in the library and in the academic classroom, with much more thought being given to the end result of the teaching process. I was convinced that we were giving more thought to identifying, and helping the reader identify, the information needs of both the student and the faculty member. I also felt that we were making far greater attempts to evaluate the work that is being done in library instruction and to analyze whether the reader's needs are being met.

I soon realized, however, that it would be very presumptuous of me to come and subject you to my own individual impression of the present state of the art in Canada without producing any supportive evidence or documentation. So I sent out a questionnaire to all the university libraries and a sampling of college libraries throughout the country. As a questionnaire it was somewhat subjective, because, obviously, I did have some preconceived impressions of the current state of the art.

1

To say that the response has been encouraging is putting it mildly because I have responses, at the moment, from all ten provinces representing close to 80% return from the questionnaire and, though the first one arrived back two days after I'd mailed it out, they are still coming in – I had a phone call yesterday asking me to stop and pick one up on the way here. But the interest in and concern for library instruction was expressed by the nature of the responses even more than by their number. I sent out a two page questionnaire (attached in a reduced format as an Appendix). People not only completed these two pages but also included letters that were not the "random thoughts on the topic" that I asked for but were very detailed and often ran to four or five pages. Several people also included sample packages of their publications and handouts.

I must say at this point how grateful I am to the people who did respond, who did take the time and who put so much thought and effort into their letters. Obviously all I'm going to be able to do today is to give a very brief dip into the mass of material I have received, picking out points that relate to my initial impressions and pin–pointing other activities that seem to be particularly interesting. I will put some of the samples out here and there should be time later for you to look at them if you are interested.

I think there are also other people in the room who can give direct comments on some of the programs that are happening in Canadian libraries. David Sharplin is here from Edmonton. Mr. Sharplin works with graduate students, especially in training graduate teaching assistants and is able to persuade instructors to be interested in library instruction. Later, I am sure Mr. Sharplin would be willing to answer anyone's questions.

I might add that, going through the questionnaires, one thing that was interesting was the number of times an idea that one person rejected as useless, or "we didn't find this to work" is the very same thing somebody else is writing about in terms of "this is the greatest thing we've come across," or "we've just begun to do this and it is really working for us." So don't take as final somebody else's failure in a particular type of project. Look closely at what they did, and why they did it on their particular campus and find out from them why it didn't work *on their campus.* I have some examples that I will quote later of things that didn't work on some campuses and *why* they didn't work. Look closely at your own campus and the people you are serving there and it might be, as some of us have obviously found, that what doesn't work for some students can work for others, because they are all different people. Every one of them is an individual with his own needs.

The main topics I covered in the survey were: *tours, publications, faculty contact, class sessions, point–of–use instruction, AV pro–*

2

grams, staff involvement in library instruction, evaluation proce-
dures, and *recent trends and future changes.* I will try to touch on
each of these briefly, quoting examples when possible, so that you
may have a feeling for what is happening, though I don't think there
is any need here to give a complete numerical analysis of all the
responses I received. Obviously I would be prepared to answer
further questions at the end on individual topics. There is a great
deal of material that is not going to be covered so feel free to ask if
I miss a particular aspect in which you are most interested.

First, a comment on the kind of universities and colleges to
which I wrote. As with the size of the institutions from which you
people come, the size of the Canadian ones varies enormously, from
the college with 330 students to the university with over 30,000. We
have a variety of mixtures of full--time and part–time students, pursuing all levels of credit and non–credit courses.

Some of our universities and most of the Quebec community
colleges face an extra challenge that most of you manage to avoid.
Librarians in universities such as Laurentian University in Ontario,
Sherbrooke and Laval in Quebec, and Moncton in New Brunswick
and in all the French language CEGEP's in Quebec have to cope with
French as well as, or instead of, English as a working language on
their campus. Many of these librarians are bilingual, many speak
only French, but they still have an extra problem in developing and
using instructional materials, especially when we are trying to share
and benefit from each other's ideas and so little of it appears in
French. Some of the responses I received, for example, included
four or five pages in French and these took a little longer to digest
than the other ones. Some of the French speaking librarians have
begun to develop very interesting programs and audio–visual presentations (as, for example, at Université de Laval in Québèc). But
now – I'll try to summarize the main topics in the survey.

TOURS: a) *General group tours*
"Showing people the library" is, I suppose, the simplistic way to
describe what most of us do when we first get into this game. Later
we go on to developing more specific ways of helping students, and
that is exactly how the programs seem to show up right across the
country. The longer an institution has had orientation programs, the
more varied and the more sophisticated they become. But all include
an introduction to the library in some form or other. Unfortunately,
too many still face the same problem as St. Michael's College in
Toronto: "The student council fall orientation program always
includes trips to the library, and we cooperate as much as we can,
but their dates, times etc. are always subject to unpredictability.
Where we can, we suggest that if student leaders are used they might

3

be from our student assistants, who are more knowledgeable than the average. I don't look on these tours as teaching much more than where we are, and how many floors we have."[2]

I should say nearly everybody implied "we are getting away from the general tour," but two thirds of those replying also said "but we do give them." This is the way we do it in the University of Toronto. We are prepared to provide tours in both the research library and the undergraduate library but first we try to encourage people to take a do-it-yourself walking tour. In the Sigmund Samual Library, we have put up the kind of graphics that hopefully make the undergraduate library self-explanatory so that most people don't need a tour, and we can concentrate on the other things. But often the faculty member is wedded to the idea that "my students must have a tour." We are trying to dissuade them from that. Many students know that they've got to get into that place called a library. They have no idea where to go once they are inside, nor what they should be doing, therefore they ask for a tour. And in some ways it's a reassuring way of saying "I don't know anything about it" and of getting the opportunity to wander around with someone else who can explain the library.

One response emphasized the need for each of us to put ourselves in the place of the student new to our campus. How often do we think back to how we felt on *our* first day on campus as we stood in one line to register, moved on to the next one to pay fees and then on again to fill out another form, feeling at the end like a sausage out of a machine – and then we went on a tour?

What did you feel like the first time you went into the University Library? (I am assuming you went in!) Do we start from that point of view when we prepare to help students use our libraries nowadays? This was brought back to me more forcibly than ever last week when I was back in the University of Edinburgh. I recalled vividly the first visit I paid to that library. After being dragged around building after building for two days we were shown the library – literally – on the Saturday afternoon. This was still the time of the century when the library closed on Saturday afternoons and there was no staff visible and it was half-dark anyway. The person who took us in said "this is not the way students normally come but, it's the fastest way from 'there' to 'here'." You know, it took me years after that to find out what the right way from there to here was! And this is the kind of thing that I feel we must remember ourselves and be aware of when we are working with the students today.

It was also interesting to notice that many Canadian librarians are now commenting that general tours are given more for pre-university groups, high-school students about to graduate and

4

people about to enter the university than for registered students. Giving this kind of tour is perceived by many as a form of publicity. We've all done it for years, but we've often said "Oh, another school tour," dumped it on the newest librarian and turned around to concentrate on the things we thought were more important. But many of the libraries that responded are including "high school tours" as one of the things which people involved in instruction and orientation consider to be a legitimate part of their work, and I think most of them felt that this is where general tours are most useful.

TOURS: b) *Self–guided printed walking tours*
Nine of the libraries that responded are now using printed sheets or booklets for self–directed or self–guided walking tours of the library. This is a type of publication with which you are all familiar, I am sure. Most of them are inconspicuous enough to let students explore the library anonymously, at their own speed, without feeling as if they were bearing huge signs to draw attention to the fact that "I'm new, I'm trying to find my way around the library." It is even possible to read such a guide ahead of one's first visit and stow it in the pocket. The walking tour usually provides a few basic facts and floor plans or a map of the buildings or other dia-- grams depending on the complexity of the building. This type of leaflet is being used to an increasing extent in Canadian libraries. Librarians are trying to help students find their own way about the building letting them identify problems for themselves as they actually use the library. In this way librarians can concentrate more on providing direct assistance when needed, either by person--to- person interviews or by point–of–use programs, publications or displays. (See also "treasure hunts" below.)

TOURS: c) *Self–guided, audio recordings*
I also checked into present use of recorded walking tours in our libraries. The people who are using this type of program successfully at the moment seem to be mainly in British Columbia -- Simon Fraser University in Burnaby and the University of British Columbia in Vancouver. At Simon Fraser there is an interesting choice between a tape which concentrates on biology, or one on the social sciences, and from that starting point students are led to different parts of the library and learn what's more relevant to their own studies. The University of Sherbrooke will be starting a French version later this year; we hope to hear more about their work this time next year.
One education library (the Faculty of Education at the Univer- sity of Toronto) reported trying these tours but no longer uses them. Though the library felt they had a very successful tape and suitable

equipment, this type of program did not meet the needs of their particular students who tend to descend on the library in hordes all on the same day with assignment--related projects. They neither had the equipment nor the space to cope with this kind of demand by means of an individual tape.

TOURS: d) *Self--guided, following signs or numbers*

Some people have tried the straight locational type of tour where you provide floor plans coded with a set of numbers that match numbers or arrows on the walls, or with coloured blocks that match coloured signs and markers indicating places where printed "legends" are posted on walls. Most people find that they would rather have a tour which is giving instruction and other information in addition to straight locations. But Concordia University in Montreal, (which some of you are more familiar with under its old name of Sir George Williams), is very successfully using a straightforward location device in addition to a variety of other programs. Queen's University uses this type "only for such events as open houses when we expect masses of outsiders who probably won't be back much."[3]

TOURS: e) *Subject--related tours*

I also asked if people were giving any subject--related tours and whether these were given at the instigation of the library, or at the instigation of the faculty members and I find that more and more libraries are in fact going this route, gearing tours and instructional visits to the library very directly to the subject matter that is being taught in the classroom.

The topics on which people give these kinds of tours vary widely across the country -- sociology, biology, geography, law, physical education, oceanography and a number of others. And when you think about it, the academic departments for which tours and introductory sessions seem to be most needed, are the ones where book resources tend to be located in a number of different places within the library building. For example, for physical education, part of that collection is in the GV's sport section and part in the science sections. Materials for oceanography, geography, and computer science is well scattered in most libraries, and more and more interdisciplinary studies are also being developed. For obvious reasons, these are all topics which present most problems for the unsophisticated library user.

In other libraries the subject--related tour is part of a larger package including on--going classroom contact. This is the situation in the Medical Library at the University of Manitoba for in--coming medical students and at Acadia for both education and divinity

6

students. In Toronto we have also had to provide special instruction for students in Biology 110 – the largest first year class in the Faculty of Arts & Science. In both Manitoba and Toronto the librarians voice a 'caveat' in relation to these programs.

"Since it should be obvious that medical students neither want to be librarians nor have need to be, it is important that teaching of bibliographic methods be oriented to medical science, not library science. It has been our experience that the easiest way to ensure that this is done, is to teach the techniques of bibliographic searching in the context of the medical curriculum, not in library isolation."[4]

The Toronto course is, in itself, an interesting development, providing the students with the opportunity for self-paced learning for most of the course, using tapes and slides. We have worked closely with the instructors and have now built a library exercise into one of the self-paced units so that not all the students hit it at the same moment and, when they do, they have to sign up for instruction if they feel they need it. This method developed from a disastrous first contact with this course which was a phone call to say "we have 2100 students doing BIO 110, can you arrange a library tour for us?" *A* library tour! We quickly converted that request to library *tours*, but even scheduling the students to come in groups of 60, and providing four staff members so that each tour had a maximum of fifteen, we seemed to be touring BIO 110 forever!

A further complication was added by the instructor whose wife was a librarian (in another library). She felt that the ability of librarians to help students with problems in specific subjects was down-graded by faculty members and unknown to students. So the task set the library was "tell the students all about what a librarian has to learn to become a librarian." And this before the students ever saw a book! It was difficult to persuade that gentleman that his students really needed to learn about resources for the biological sciences before they tackled library science! Since then, with the experience of that year, we have arranged a session each year with the faculty as they begin preparing the course, and have, as mentioned above, inserted a library element as part of one of the self-paced learning units of the course.

The frustration of the first year was, therefore, worth pursuing, and this also shows up in the response from a number of other institutions who have faced similar situations. The message is clear – don't give up because the first contact with a faculty member, or with a student, or with a class does not seem to be successful. Be sure you sit down afterwards and really analyze what succeeded, what was non-productive, and why? The second year will be easier, but by then you will have been recommended to other departments on campus, and they will all be expecting the same treatment. So,

7

beware, the more success we generate with our programs, the more prepared we have to be to repeat or do a similar program for other academic departments.

PUBLICATIONS:
On the questionnaire I asked about types of publications, for whom prepared and whether or not a charge was imposed. Many are still available without charge, but with tight budgets this is an activity that will obviously be affected. In fact, those libraries which have begun to charge for publications have found that this gives a greater value to the publication because, as you know yourself, people sometimes have more respect for something they pay for than for anything that is given away free. One library even commented that from now on they are never going to publish anything printed on one side of the page with a blank page on the back because they found that when they did this their publications were being used as scrap paper. It almost seemed as if the blank side of the paper was of more interest to the students than the printed side. Now they are putting out everything double-sided and obviously are saving a great deal of paper!

The more complex bibliographies (and more of these are being published right across the country) are the ones which tend to have had a cost attached from the beginning. In some cases they are distributed free on their own campus and sold to others. In other cases there is a charge to everybody. Some libraries have an interesting philosophy about that, though. There is at least one campus where there is a bulk sale to an academic department of an item that is directly relevant to that department. That department is then responsible for picking up the cost and for dealing with distribution or sale to their own students. In some places this also gives the kind of authority to a publication that picking it up at the library desk doesn't.

One other cost-saving device is employed by the University of Manitoba. They transfer the whole cost of a publication directly to the student by having only one copy of each bibliography available for consultation. It is, however, also available for "photocopy at reader's expense."

One comment made by Hilari Anderson at Concordia University is one about which we should all be doing more thinking in relation to publications whether they are leaflets, brochures or books. "Be very careful about the title you attach to a publication." She has had an identical handout with two titles. When it was called "The Card Catalogue" it sat . . . in a heap. Once it was re-named "How to Find a Book" it has been going "like hot cakes." Text and layout are identical but the response is quite different!

8

I have some samples I'd like to use briefly, to give you an idea of the type, format and scope of items being put out by Canadian libraries. Library handbooks come in all shapes and sizes, and in two different languages, from the libraries that still publish them. More and more have changed to a different format or have ceased to produce a handbook at all, because of lack of funds and, often, also because of lack of interest on the part of the reader. One or two have been designed for specific purposes. One is purely and simply a folder punched for a three ring binder. Entitled "From A to Z," it gives everything you should want to know about the Library at the University of Saskatchewan with a blank timetable in front. It can be used on its own as a ready reference tool or can be used as the cover within which the reader collects other single sheet handouts dealing in greater detail with specific aspects of library use or with individual library services. More and more libraries are going the route of Saskatchewan and Carleton University and splitting all the basic information about the library into small parts which the reader collects as the need arises. It is obvious that a great deal of thought and planning has gone into these sets, many of which are colour-coded and look very attractive. It is also clear that many are economically produced, using coloured papers and one ink, using regular duplicating equipment which is probably found in the library.

Others, such as one from the University of Calgary pack a great deal of information on one eye-catching page or one bookmark. The students respond very favorably to the attractive Calgary one. I would be less happy receiving my introduction to the library in an 8½" x 14" format, closely typed and unillustrated, particularly when the title on the front is "Around the Library in 120 Minutes." That may well be suitable for the students for whom it was designed but it certainly wouldn't satisfy ours! The University of Saskatchewan has a catchy title for its series, "The understanding-in-one-minute-series" and, to those of us who have seen it, the series title implies that a student is more likely to look at that than the 120-minute one!

Another eye-catching item is the handbook from the University of British Columbia (UBC). It is a beautiful piece of printing with an intriguing design linking front and back covers. The layout and format in themselves arouse comment and interest and encourage people to look inside though there again one finds a fairly solidly printed text. The basic question with this material as with the 120-minute item, is "how much do we need to tell at any one time?"

Concordia has material whose layout, catchy titles and illustrations quickly get the attention of both faculty and students. One is called *The Owner's Manual*, and it is just that. It is well laid out and the contribution of a graphic artist is very clear in this publication.

It looks expensive, but I am assured that the heavy brown paper used is, in fact, a cheap grade, recycled paper. Another feature contributing to its success is the originality and ingenuity in the headings. A glossary of library terms is billed as "the library decoded." Also, once you find your book, the page headed, "how long can I keep it?" leaves no doubt about the length of your loan, and the heading, "what should I do if it's not in the stacks?" sums up the clear message of that page. Not all of us have the resources to produce this book, but there are ideas in the approach taken that we might all use.

I think Concordia and UBC are the only places with graphic artists actually on the library staff. But there are many other places where there are graphic artists somewhere on campus, and most of us don't make use of them. Not all of us can afford the rates they charge, but that is a question we all have to fight out on our own campus. Various academic departments in Toronto have graphic artists. The cost often seems prohibitive, but there are times when the first priority is a professional production. Often we have found much of our artistic talents among library staff and student assistants.

As an aside, it is interesting to note the comment from Joan Sandilands in British Columbia "that our graphic artist is busier and needs more assistance each year is significant – posters, instructional displays, etc., are becoming more important."[5]

Another type of publication being used in a number of Canadian libraries bears some relation to a walking tour but goes beyond the geographical layout of the building to teach a bit more about the actual use of the library by leading the student through a learning experience. This takes various forms but basically consists of a workbook type of publication, often giving a programmed-learning approach to use of catalogs, etc., often creating a "treasure hunt" to make a game out of locating a book, often using the "Library Experience" format (described elsewhere in this volume by Richard Dewey) to introduce the student to the literature on a specific subject.

Some of these workbooks are quite simple in both content and format. One from Queen's University called "Library treasure hunt" combines a compact size (8½" x 5") with large type. It suggests a particular author or title for a student to follow through to the end of the process of locating the book. On each page it gives one simple instruction or one reassuring message. It sets an informal and en--couraging tone from the very first page and was so successful that, on the first occasion these were used, over 1500 students quickly found their book and a lollipop within six hours! That was one gimmick that went over very well without enormous expense ($80 including booklets and lollipops) and it also generated the atmosphere that library wanted to create with its student body. I gather that other people have used more expensive gifts at the end, but the lollipops were enough to break down the reserve between student and librarian.

More and more, I think, people are turning towards this type of publication. The one from the University of Western Ontario is larger and sells for 35 cents. It is a programmed-learning workbook on the use of the catalog. The student is presented with a set of possible answers to each question, with directions to go to a different page for whichever answer is selected. This takes more time for the student to complete, but the library has now used it successfully for several years. The students like it. There is also a gimmick built into this on the front cover. The title depends on how you interpret the pictogram on the front: is it the "Great Lakes Fishy Story" or the "Great Lakes Fish Story?" This does start people talking about it before they even open the cover.

A couple of libraries refer to Mimi Dudley's *Workbook in Library Skills*, which is described more fully elsewhere in this volume. Neither Sherbrooke nor Windsor, however, indicate how they are using the book, or if they are planning to use it. It is not clear whether it has been used merely as a reference tool for the librarian, or used extensively by the student body.

From almost all provinces I have received samples of *Pathfinders* or similar one-page introductions to the literature for a specific topic. McMaster has its *Searchlights*. The University of British Columbia uses *Start Here*'s. In other places there are various series, such as *Introduction to . . .* and so on. Some librarians express a dislike of this type of material, but most seem to feel that, with a careful introduction explaining their scope, these can be very helpful to students, and reduce repetitive questions at information desks.

Remember, try to be original in your publications, but if you *are* borrowing somebody else's ideas, give credit to those from whom you borrow, for example, *Pathfinder* material, or material on how to find periodical articles. I found that one booklet, *How to Review a Book*, is being used by a number of libraries across the country though not all of them have given credit where credit seems to be due. Some publications claim to be "based on" one by Ashley Thompson. Others say "by Ashley Thompson" -- a few give no credit at all, but it's very clear where the idea came from and it is also clear that Ashley Thompson has been in more than one library because he replied to me from Laurentian this year. He was previously in Saskatchewan. It is interesting to see where people move by the way programs change from year to year. Use other people's

11

ideas, pick their brains, but share the fact that you have done it (preferably *with* the original author!) -- then you can go on a step further. Don't try to re-invent the wheel -- go on to the next step. Build on someone else's work and at least give them the credit when you use their ideas; possibly you can also share with them the way you have developed the idea.

Before leaving publications, I should make a couple of brief comments. Don't ignore "freebies" and check out commercially produced material. Some of the leaflets and booklets available from time to time free from publishers and library supply companies almost amount to "Point of Use" instruction (see also p.15). Several libraries do report distributing such items as how to use *Science Citations Index, Readers' Guide*, etc. Others use books like Campbell and Lupton: *The Canadian Student's Guide to Research*,[6] to introduce search strategies to beginners.

CLASSROOM AND FACULTY CONTACT:

Not all of us are able to establish the kind of rapport with the classroom teacher that the Rev. Charles Brewer, librarian at St. Francis Xavier University, in Nova Scotia, seems to have achieved.

"We arrange with professors of all first-year students in English, History, Sociology and Psychology to have from two to three meetings with their class. These meetings are held early in October when assignments have started to force them to use the library. We follow up the classroom meetings with a tour of the library for each of these classes." (Total enrollment approximately 2200.)

One of the biggest differences between our institutions nowadays is whether or not there is any compulsory component common to all undergraduate programs. Some universities and most community colleges still have compulsory English classes for first year students and at least one institution, Université de Moncton, has "francais obligatoire." This situation presents an opportunity to the librarian to provide library instruction. This is done at the University of British Columbia, and at Victoria, Laurentian, Moncton and at most community colleges. At Seneca College and the University of Calgary a similar situation exists, with a different twist to it: all new students in business courses have a library session as a required part of their course.

To have a direct channel into one of the academic departments through which everyone must go is obviously a gift that we shouldn't ignore. Those librarians who make use of this channel usually visit the classroom, conduct library related activities including a tour and often work with the professor in developing worksheets. At UBC, for example, "the session consists of an 8-minute slide/tape show explaining the library system in general, a 20-minute lecture on

12

basic research techniques, and a brief tour of Sedgewick. Our aim in this program is not 'to explain it all' but to give beginning students some idea of the resources the library has to offer and to let them know that there are people in the library who can help them find what they need."[7] At the University of Victoria, a shift is planned soon from tours to programmed instruction (printed text) for first year English courses.

We also have a number of universities such as Toronto and Mount Allison where there are now no compulsory English or French courses and where individual learning and study projects are encouraged. Some librarians lamented the disappearance of compulsory courses which often represented an "open door" to the classroom. In fact, what has happened is an increased awareness of the need for library instruction by faculty members in other disciplines. Librarians have thus been given the opportunity and the incentive to diversify programs, publications and other forms of publicity. They also have more classes to which the student comes on a voluntary basis, thus providing for a more rewarding experience for both librarian and student.

There are some universities which are still in the happy position of having a small enough faculty that the Library can get in touch with every faculty member who is new to the campus. At places like St. Michael's College in Toronto, and McMaster University in Hamilton, they invite all the new faculty members in to the Library. At McMaster, they meet the Chief Librarian and they each have a personal orientation to the library. At Simon Fraser University and others, groups of new faculty members are invited to a social hour. This coud be one of the benefits of tighter budgets if every university appoints fewer and fewer new faculty members each year. It is up to us to find out who the new people are because soon, it seems, there will not be many of them even in the larger institutions. We should try to devise ways of ensuring that we get them to the library and try to have them on the Library's side before they meet their students.

CLASS SESSIONS SPONSORED BY LIBRARIANS:
There's only one place in Canada that I'm aware of which offers a credit course in library skills -- Wilfrid Laurier University in Ontario. Sherbrooke is preparing to include a credit course in their new program; a number of other librarians are also considering credit courses. The Rev. Erich Schultz, the librarian at Wilfred Laurier, was the only person to send a description of a course that has actually been used.

Non-credit courses, in particular the kind for which students sign up voluntarily to receive help in writing papers (term paper clinics, etc.) are conducted at places like Windsor, York and Toronto. The Toronto course has had various names such as "Two Steps Towards a Better Essay" but always requires the completion of a worksheet and an individual session with a librarian.

The class sessions include one by a faculty member from one of the University's Writing Laboratories. These sessions began on Saturdays and evenings and have now also spread to other days of the week because of their success. It has been obvious that the students were receptive to this program, but it was encouraging recently to have one of the University's senior administrators comment that he was hearing great things about the work the library was doing to help students with their essays.

Windsor has redesigned their non-credit course "Bibliography One" as a six-week, four-session course to be repeated regularly, *at a cost to the student* of $6.00 for materials. Several other libraries such as Rimouski in Quebec and the University of Western Ontario are considering the development of credit courses. All in all, there is a definite move away from the "hit and run" type of instruction, such as one class and one tour, towards the teaching of research strategies with follow-up counselling.

Brescia College in London, also has an interesting new program beginning in September 1976 when, "with our present library staff, and teaching faculty, a new faculty member, who is a qualified teacher and librarian, will attempt to develop a program of library research skills for preliminary and first year students."[8]

At the University of New Brunswick faculty cooperation takes the form of having faculty member and librarian jointly *in class* going over a library quiz which the student has completed and corrected for himself.

Much of the faculty contact depends on library publicity and public relations and on the means used by both librarians and faculty members to motivate students to use libraries.

LIBRARY PUBLICITY:

Simon Fraser University uses a simple device to keep the library in the forefront in the community by including a library message in the postage meter so that all university mail carries a "free" message.

A great deal of work is being done on campuses across the country to sell library programs both to faculty members and to students, by direct contacts, by informal invitations, and by producing more and more publications that are simple but eye-catching to try and turn the attention of the campus to the library. At least two libraries, Concordia University and Dawson College in Montreal, publish a library newsletter that goes all around campus giving library news, or have a library column in the university's newspaper.

Others take advantage of any opportunity they can. At Guelph they even had a games booth sponsored by the library on a student carnival night. The booth featured LC call numbers and subject headings and apparently it was very popular and brought the library program to the attention of the students and the campus as a whole.

One of the things we try in a number of libraries is to ease that first entrance into an academic library by deliberately trying to break down some of the hurdles that seem to intimidate the new student. I can use Toronto again as an example of this. At the start of each academic term we put a coffee pot in the entrance hall of the undergraduate library. Most students and faculty appreciate the prominent sign welcoming them to the university or to a new term and, with it, the invitation to a free cup of coffee. Some don't stop for the coffee until they are on the way out, and often ask: "Does the sign really mean what it says?" But after they do fill a cup, they have to stand there for at least five minutes while they drink it! To take advantage of this, we also make a point of mounting various instructional displays in the foyer, beyond which they may not carry the coffee! We also have all our library publications available there and have librarians sitting right there looking as if they have nothing to do and, therefore, appearing free to talk. This has been a very productive and relatively inexpensive way to create good relations with the student body.

From time to time during the year we mount further instructional displays such as 'What a *Pathfinder* is, and how it can help you use the library better and write better essays,' at the same locations.

Many of us use direct mail to faculty members, and at Guelph the library also makes use of bulk mail to students in residence. Other means of advertising over campus radio stations and by posters, fliers, etc. were mentioned repeatedly.

One of the most successful publications directed towards bringing students into the library has to be the *Light-Hearted Guide to the Douglas Library Plus its Services* which provides students at Queen's with "everything you always wanted to know about the library but were afraid to ask" in the form of newspaper ads and classifieds. How many other campuses bill their archives as "For the Truly Unique in Non-Books" or have "New Stock Arriving Daily" in the Periodicals Room?

POINT-OF-USE INSTRUCTION:

Recently a number of people seem to have increased their emphasis and reliance on specific point-of-use instruction. As mentioned before, some are using the publisher's material for *Science Citation Index, Readers' Guide*, etc., placing a bundle of the leaflets beside copies of the book. This has been happening in a number of places. Others have made displays of particular reference tools and how to use them. Guelph University Library is in the process at the moment of setting up what is called an *Orientation Room* where there will be a number of reference tools available with explanatory devices telling people what the books are used for, how they can be used and where they are shelved. It is felt from experiments done as a preparation, that this kind of situation will be useful for their students. The student can browse around the room, try to use the material at his own speed and then come to ask questions about it rather than being told all about it when he isn't yet ready to know anything about it.

A-V PRESENTATIONS:

About half the libraries responding include some form of audiovisual material in their programs. In turn they seem to be almost equally devided between tape-slide programs giving a general orientation to the library, and specific point-of-use programs. Those who define the type mostly refer to tape-slide, and the variety described by Audrey Turner from Ottawa seems to cover the most common of these: "Finding and Borrowing Library Materials, Card Catalog, Finding Periodical Articles." Point-of-use programs include both institutionally produced and commercially available productions. In Toronto we are now using tape-slide, videotape and transparencies. There are a number of programs now related to specific tools for studies in scientific or medical subjects. Toronto programs include video-tapes on *MEDLINE* and "Getting it Together" (term paper on pollution), and tape-slide programs on "Guide to the Literature of Medicine and Related Subjects," "Guide to Abstracting and Indexing Services," "Science Citation Index," "CINL -- Cumulative Index to Nursing Literature," "Beilstein," and "Guide to the Use of Chemical Abstracts." These programs are now being catalogued by the University's Media Center and included in their AV catalogs. This should make these productions available to a much wider audience. Several of the programs are adaptations of material from the Institute of Scientific Information in Philadelphia – again, with permission and with credit being given on an extra slide.

STAFF INVOLVEMENT IN LIBRARY INSTRUCTION:

There are signs that more and more university administrators are becoming aware of *and* acknowledging the role that the library instruction program plays in the whole life of the campus. This aspect is particularly important when we are all operating under such tight budget constraints. The question that was asked earlier this morning about what happens to library instruction if your institution has to face a 10% cut is a significant one. Few institutions are free from that kind of threat. The interesting thing that shows up from the questionnaires is that, perhaps because of this kind of question, library instruction programs continue to be developed so that they will meet the needs of the student. Library instruction is beginning to play a more vital role in the whole academic process than it has in the past.

Obviously we will have to evaluate what we have been doing and provide justification for what we plan to do to an extent that is new to most of us. We also have to continue the often frustrating task of trying to make both students and faculty members assess their needs for library instruction and of persuading them that we can, in the library, offer something to fill these needs. As a real assessment of priorities takes place it seems that library instruction programs have a good chance of improving and of growing rather than shrinking in spite of the budget or possibly because of the need to be so budget conscious.

There seem to be about six Canadian universities with a full time person responsible for the library instruction/library orientation programs. UBC has an Information and Orientation Division with three librarians, one library assistant and one graphic artist. This Division was established in 1968 before most of the other libraries made full time appointments. Now, however, there are a number of others where people report "we hope soon to have a full-time person" and several others where someone spends three-quarter time on library instruction.

In places where there is nobody devoting their full time to library instruction the responsibility is often shared by all the reference librarians, by individual volunteers or even by the Chief Librarian in smaller institutions.

In almost all the libraries where there is a full-time appointment, and in several others, there are committees actively engaged in planning and developing library instruction. These vary in composition between staff from all public service departments and staff from all departments in the library. Some committees include students, others have representatives of the various group of users. Among places with widely representative committees are UBC, Saskatchewan, McMaster, Toronto and Laval.

SOME TRENDS:

A renewed emphasis on the use of good teaching techniques and on the need for improvement in teaching standards both in libraries and in the wider academic setting is clear from many of the responses. Carleton University in Ottawa has library staff involved in giving courses that are set up by the University to improve teaching; at Sherbrooke there is a similar situation. At Dalhousie

University in Nova Scotia a committee has been formed this year on improving teaching in the University and they have shown an interest in the library's instruction programs. I was at a meeting yesterday in Toronto discussing the Ontario Universities' Program on Instructional Development. This program has been going for a couple of years now and has been giving direct grants to encourage improved and innovative teaching, but it has concentrated on people teaching in the academic classroom.

The terms of reference now include not only academic teaching but also "improved student learning" as the first goal of the program. This would seem to open the door wide for involvement by librarians throughout Ontario, but first we will have to ensure that each of our campuses is aware of what we are doing. We should also be taking every opportunity to upgrade librarians' teaching skills as is being done in the University of Manitoba where "two of the reference staff were registered in half-day, two-week *In-Service for University Professors' Programs* given by the Faculty of Education. These programs provide instruction in teaching skills, timing of presentations, and course construction."[9]

One other important thing that is happening is that more and more institutions have been working on goals and objectives and are really taking a close look at all their activities related to instruction in library use. Several have drawn up a coordinated program to meet all the needs and some are now working on future planning. At Laurentian they have established a three-tier program to meet the needs of different categories and levels of library users. At Toronto we have tried to tie together the goals of each individual part of our program and are now looking at ways of improving our advance planning. Sherbrooke has prepared a complete listing of a new program which they have planned as a whole package including an introductory course for faculty members as part of their whole orientation program.

Throughout almost all the responses there is mention of a growing interest in and involvement with evaluation of programs. The proposed Sherbrooke program has an evaluation process built in and their report should make interesting reading (in French) sometime in late 1977. The variety of evaluation methods being used now include questionnaires, worksheets and library quizzes such as those used at Laurentian as a test after basic library instruction.

I'd like to make two final comments on cooperation with library schools and on the role of Canadian library organizations and other ad-hoc groups in library instruction.

More and more people are reporting contacts with library schools and use of library school students in library instruction programs. In UBC, library school staff and students help with term paper clinics.

In Toronto, staff at the Faculty of Library Science include in the Reference courses the preparation of library *Pathfinders* geared to the topics about which we are asked questions at the information desk in the undergraduate library. We give the professor our long list of topics for which we still need *Pathfinders* and these are offered for library school students to choose as part of their assignments. A number of libraries have involved students in this way, by providing as topics for assignments questions for which the library needs answers or subjects on which it needs instructional programs.

On our national level the work that has been done by the Canadian Library Association's (CLA) Committee on Orientation seems to come to life about every four years when it sponsors a workshop or other program. The first two or three were similar to "show and tell" programs that have been held at ALA. There was a program in Toronto in the early sixties, one in Newfoundland in 1969, and last year in Toronto the Canadian Association of College and University Libraries co-sponsored a set of pre-conference workshops dealing with various aspects of orientation and instruction in library use. Last year and in 1969 bibliographies were prepared for the workshops to add to what a former chairman of the CLA committee describes as "the stream of bibliographies and information packages that have been produced and placed, I believe, in an archives/clearing house that was established some years ago."[10]

For a number of years now the library at the Association of Universities and Colleges of Canada, in Ottawa, has maintained and circulated collections of printed material on library instruction, including handbooks, etc., in much the same way that the library of the American Library Association does.

Throughout the country various groups of librarians get together from time to time to share their common interest in instruction in library use. After a workshop here, five of us from Canada formed an ad-hoc steering committee to organize a *Workshop: Instruction in Library Use*. This event is now in its fifth year. For each Workshop we set a theme, so next week sixty academic librarians from Ontario and Quebec meeting in Kingston will concentrate on planning and evaluating library instruction. In British Columbia there is an organization (TRIUL) representing the three university libraries in the province and the regional community colleges. They meet annually to discuss matters of common concern, usually including library instruction.

In Ontario we also have an Orientation Information Exchange. For this we take advantage of the Inter-University Transit Service which links the provincial Universities. There is a box that is nearly always on the move from Orientation Librarian to Orientation Librarian or from Reference Department to Reference Department.

In this box there is a section for each library and a few general sections. When anybody produces a new publication or program they put one copy or information about it in the section for each of the other universities. People can also put in questions and on the way round somebody else usually provides an answer or adds further comments or suggestions. The box doesn't go round very quickly, it doesn't go round very often, but it is a good way of keeping in touch with what is going on. The librarians of the Quebec Community Colleges (CEGEP) meet together about once a year and instruction in library use is also one of the topics they discuss. I understand that various other local groups get together from time to time independently or under the auspices of one of the provincial library associations. None of the responses to the questionnaire suggested that there was any great desire to have a regular national gathering on this topic. It seems that Canadian librarians still feel the greatest value lies in meeting regionally, as frequently as possible, with groups and individuals who are involved in this same task of helping library patrons and potential patrons to make full use of library resources and services. There is continued interest in occasional functions sponsored on the national level by the Canadian Library Association but the attraction of a more frequent local event seems to be stronger.

All in all, we've come a long way in Canadian academic libraries since the mid-60's when Gene Gattinger almost stole the show in New York with his description of some of the problems he'd met in Newfoundland including students who couldn't understand how to use catalogs as "My mother always taught me never to open anybody else's drawers." This year's reply from Memorial University would imply that this problem no longer exists!

But in many ways the message that Verna Melum gave to one of the early Ypsilanti conferences is still true, at least in Canadian libraries. The first essentials are to let the student know where the library is and that the staff are prepared to help and really *do* want people to use their books. To get *that* across to all students, is still the greatest challenge facing us, but there is so much more that is happening now which must add to the satisfaction students derive from their studies and librarians find in their work.

NOTES

1. CEGEP is the abbreviation for the Colleges d'enseignment general et professional in Quebec, and is the term by which they are commonly and collectively known.

2. Margaret McGrath, personal letter. Toronto, April 30, 1976.

3. Sandra Arendt, personal letter. Kingston, April, 1976.

4. Audrey M. Kerr "Medical Library, University of Manitoba – additional comments to questionnaire." p. 1.

5. Joan Sandilands, personal letter. Vancouver, April 13, 1976.

6. Samual S. Campbell and Nora Lupton, *The Canadian Student's Guide to Research*. (Don Mills, Ont., General Publishing, 1974) paperback. $1.95.

7. Joan Sandilands, "Description of responsibilities of the Information and Orientation Division in the University of British Columbia Library," 1975. p. 1.

8. Sister Pierina Caverzan, personal letter. London, May 4, 1976.

9. Kathryn Dean, "Report on student orientation -- Elizabeth Dafoe Library, University of Manitoba." p. 2.

10. Garth Homer, personal letter. Aberystwyth, Wales, May 12, 1976.

GENERAL NOTE:

I have not covered instruction in the use of computer data bases or microform catalogs or automated services other than as they occur in the regular programs covered. Many Canadian libraries are involved with such services, but most are in the early stages or developing instructional tools and programs for both staff and students. I anticipate many developments within the near future on this.

APPENDIX

CONDENSED FORMAT:
Omits mailing information and space for answers!

QUESTIONNAIRE ON LIBRARY INSTRUCTION
AND ORIENTATION

Name and title and institution of person completing

1. What forms of library instruction and orientation are used in your library? Please describe the types you use, as listed below, and add any others not mentioned. Please describe as fully as possible, using a separate sheet if necessary.

Format	*Time of Year & Frequency*	*Types Or Topics*	*For What Audience?*

1a) *Tours*   i) General:

  ii) Related to specific subjects:

  iii) Self-guided -- printed

  iv) Self-guided -- following signs or numbers (clues posted throughout the library)

1b) *Publications* (e.g. maps, handbooks, worksheets, *Pathfinders*, bibliographies)

  i) Free?

  ii) For a cost? To whom?

  iii) Workbooks -- self-correcting
       librarian-correcting
       faculty member correcting

1c) *Meetings with Faculty Members* For specific disciplines? In general?

  i) Informal -- how arranged?

  ii) Formal -- when? and how arranged?

1d) *Class Sessions* -- Related to specific academic subjects:

                               Credit/Noncredit   One Time/Series

       i) Librarian visiting class

       ii) Class or section visiting library

1e) *Class sessions* -- Sponsored by Library (or others?) -- essay clinics, bibliographic instr. etc.

       Credit/non-credit? ....   One time/Series? ....

1f) *Point-Of-Use Instruction* by i) Displays (e.g. Indexes)?
                                     ii) A-V presentations?

1g) *Do You Use A-V Programs* For Any Other Instructional Purposes?

2.   Are any of the activities covered in question 1 compulsory for any students or faculty members on your campus? If so, which? and for whom?

3.   Do any librarians or other members of your library staff have a full-time responsibility for orientation/instruction? How many of each category?

4.   Is orientation carried out by staff of one department (e.g. reference)?

5.   Is there a committee to plan instruction and orientation programs? Is it library-wide in representation? Does it have or seek input from students and/or faculty members?

6.   How do you publicize programs?

7.   Have you any evaluation procedures built into, or following the programs you conduct?

8.   Do you see any significant changes in the type, format and/or role of instruction in library use on your campus?

9.   Have there been any significant trends in recent years related to library instruction on your campus?

THANK YOU FOR YOUR HELP -- AND PLEASE FEEL
FREE TO ADD ANYTHING ELSE THAT YOU THINK
MAY BE WORTH SHARING.

THE STATUS OF PROJECT LOEX

Carolyn Kirkendall
Project LOEX Director
Eastern Michigan University

At the first of what were to become annual library orientation conferences here at Eastern Michigan University, the idea for a national orientation clearinghouse was conceived. By 1972, the exchange, called Project LOEX, was a working reality. With the announcement in January of 1975 of a three-year grant awarded to LOEX by the Council on Library Resources, our exchange received an official assurance of continuing activity and support.

As most of you know, LOEX stands for Library Orientation and Instruction Exchange. We are a national – even international -- clearinghouse. Our primary objective is to collect, organize and disseminate information and materials relating to academic library orientation and instruction. We also aid libraries in their research endeavors in the field, encourage the sharing of both materials and information among other kinds of agencies and committees involved with instruction, and promote and publicize the development of library instruction whenever and wherever we can.

Since LOEX reported to you at last year's conference, our workload has increased a great deal. Any credit we could claim for expanded office services lies directly with you and with all the registered LOEX member libraries and other library friends involved with instruction. Without the contribution of materials and information, and without the interest, support, and continuing contact with us, LOEX would be an idle office. We very much appreciate the splendid cooperation which we receive, and through which we exist. Though we do express our gratitude in an occasional issue of LOEX News, this conference seems a most appropriate occasion to say thank you officially.

The following statistics will illustrate just how busy we've been this past year. These figures will also serve as springboards for elaborating each area of office activity, and for sharing with you some considerations and potential areas of concern in library instruction today.

	As of Dec. 1974	As of May 1975	As of Dec. 1975	As of May 1976
Materials in Collection	1,261	1,500	3,834	5,117

To point out some generalized trends in the production of library instruction materials during the past year, I can report that LOEX is receiving more course and lecture outlines, more collections of exercises and textbooks, more printed self-guided tours, more post-tests, pre-tests, pathfinders, program descriptions and guides to research than apparently previously produced. Libraries seem to be producing fewer bibliographies, shorter handbooks, conducting fewer escorted library tours, and publishing more library guides in loose-leaf format. There continues to be an expanded involvement with media in teaching library use.

LOEX encourages you to continue to contribute sample materials which your library produces. At one time, librarians seemed more reticent to deposit what they probably considered to be just average samples, but we assure you that all contributions continue to be of value for use in the LOEX collection.

Our selection of actual media samples is expanding, and any program which is donated to LOEX is valuable. If any of you have sample scripts of audio-visual productions, please mail us one copy; even a rough draft will suffice. We continue to put all sample scripts to good and immediate use in filling requests to examine these items.

	As of Dec. 1974	As of May 1975	As of Dec. 1975	As of May 1976
Members	240	258	442	487
Friends	–	--	--	119

The next category of figures represents actual membership count. An academic library automatically becomes a LOEX member when they return a completed membership questionnaire to our office. We have just revised our questionnaire for the second time since last May, and will continue to attempt to improve and adapt it. Members outside of the continental United States who have joined our exchange during the past year include libraries from Hawaii, Nigeria, Puerto Rico, the Virgin Islands, Peru, Columbia, Italy, and sixteen Canadian members.

This year we have added an additional statistic – that of LOEX "friends." These are libraries or individual librarians who borrow our materials, request to receive the *LOEX News*, represent national library instruction committees, and others. We also do a small selective soliciting for libraries to become members or friends. When we hear of a particular library instruction program which interests us, at an institution which is not in contact with us, we will initiate the relationship, and have received in almost all instances an immediate and positive reponse.

	As of Dec. 1974	As of May 1975	As of Dec. 1975	As of May 1976
Requests for Information	64	80	274	293

The fourth category of statistics is requests for information. This is the area that LOEX is all about, and the area which demands the most time and energy, and is, by far, the most interesting and vital activity for our office.

Having received more requests so far this year than the total number of contacts last year, the number 293 reflects the interest and flurry of activity which library instruction is receiving. It's really a significant figure, because each request which LOEX receives indicates either a new program being developed or an ongoing program being revised, or another individual librarian who considers library instruction to be a worthwhile and necessary component of library service.

Some requests may take LOEX several days to answer; others are relatively simple to fill. Unfortunately, LOEX cannot furnish answers to some of the requests we receive – a frustrating experience. That is when we advertise in *LOEX News* for information and samples from you. We've been asked, for example, for figures on budget allocations for library instruction programs, and we do not have such a category in our questionnaire to collect these figures. Statistics on released time for teaching library credit courses are not available from the LOEX data bank. Samples of library instruction for the visually handicapped and for the provisionally-accepted or low-achiever student are also sparse, and a further example of a request which LOEX, at the time, could not adequately fill.

When LOEX is confronted with requests for materials which are not in our collection, we often personally solicit for them. A request for sample guides to Instructional Materials Centers or Curriculum Laboratories has resulted in LOEX contacting each academic library that had indicated, in a handbook or library guide, that such a separate library division existed. We've used the same procedure to expand our collection of printed programmed materials.

Each time that LOEX receives a request and compiles a list for a particular kind of library instruction program or activity, we add this data to our files, and continue to expand and revise all lists as new information is received.

	As of Dec. 1974	As of May 1975	As of Dec. 1975	As of May 1976
Requests to Receive LOEX NEWS & to Join LOEX:	–	61	136	63

LOEX also has been keeping a count of how many requests our office receives asking to be added to the mailing list for the quarterly publication, *LOEX News*, or inquiring how one can participate in our national exchange. At present, *LOEX News* is mailed to approximately 700 academic libraries and individuals.

	As of Dec. 1974	As of May 1975	As of Dec. 1975	As of May 1976
Exhibits:	–	2	14	5

LOEX provides traveling exhibits of selected sample materials for large conferences and meetings, on a first-come, first-served basis. We mail all exhibit displays through UPS, and request that the materials be returned in the same fashion as quickly as possible, so that LOEX can honor all commitments for exhibits. We will be happy to compile exhibits in any area of orientation and instruction for a specialized meeting.

	As of Dec. 1974	As of May 1975	As of Dec. 1975	As of May 1976
Letters Written:	–	64	251	298

Not counting the letters accompanying any materials or research assignments which LOEX has filled, this line of statistics represents the additional correspondence LOEX has completed. These figures further emphasize the growing interest in bibliographic instruction programs today.

	As of Dec. 1974	As of May 1975	As of Dec. 1975	As of May 1976
Circulation:	342	75	3795	2150

At least one-third to one-half of the LOEX collection of sample materials is in constant circulation. The actual count represents the expanded LOEX office service as well as the expanded interest in examining a wide variety of library instruction materials produced by others.

	As of Dec. 1974	As of May 1975	As of Dec. 1975	As of May 1976
LOEX News:	2	1	4	1

This final line of statistics indicates how many issues of *LOEX News* have been published, and that the newsletter is now issued as a quarterly. The *News* is the only channel of communication, other than personal letter, which LOEX uses to relay information and share new developments in the orientation/instruction field. We continue to request your participation and input, so that the publication will reflect current and comprehensive views.

On a temporary, experimental basis, LOEX publicizes the availability of several compilations which our office completed. These lists included: computer-assisted instruction programs; handbooks and library guides produced for faculty; library-sponsored term paper clinics and sample materials; library instruction in the use of government documents; and printed programmed materials produced for bibliographic instruction. In the last six weeks, we have received 197 requests for copies of one or more of these lists – additional evidence that a national exchange can be and is used, and that the widespread interest in library instruction continues to expand.

For a quick report in a few selected areas, you will be interested in learning that, according to LOEX data, there are now thirteen libraries utilizing computer-assisted instruction, seventy-seven libraries utilizing video-tape to teach the use of library tools and to orient the user to physical layout and services, and 218 libraries which are using or producing slide/tape presentations in their library orientation and instruction programs.

From this summarized report, you now have a somewhat detailed picture of how LOEX operates, what kinds of services we can provide, and which sorts of activities and demands keep our office hopping. You can also correctly surmise that Library Instruction is, indeed, alive and well and living practically everywhere.

You can also surmise, from the statistics we've discussed today, that this expansion of activity could also indicate that we may have created our own kind of monster.

LOEX would probably not be able to continue to provide adequate and comprehensive service if some of these figures would double in about a year's time. However, there is a solution, and a way you can all help. There are at present twenty-two local, state and regional library instruction clearinghouses established or developing. This figure also includes committees and individuals from states not formally organized. If your state is not represented by an area agency, LOEX encourages you to return home from this conference to establish your own organization. And LOEX, in turn, promises to provide all kinds of samples and advice on how to do so.

If each area or state clearinghouse would survey library instruction programs of their regional academic libraries, collect information and samples, organize this data and materials, publish a directory of these activities, and provide LOEX with a copy of this summary, then our own assignment of collecting and disseminating on a national level would be greatly alleviated, and a comprehensive, current and truly national representation of library orientation and instruction would be readily available to anyone.

I think this procedure is the only answer for our kind of central exchange. Please consider participating, if you are interested in helping to advance academic library instruction and to maintain its integral role in the total library service program. This will need to be done if a representative national clearinghouse such as ours can continue to operate effectively.

One major consideration in library instruction today needs to be emphasized. The larger the LOEX collection grows, the larger the potential problem also looms. The more samples we circulate, the more we need to address ourselves to this concern. LOEX urges all users and borrowers of any sample materials produced by any academic library and donated to our collection to keep in mind that no material can be adopted, adapted, or modified without citing the original producing institution. While almost all of the 5,000+ materials contributed to LOEX are to be shared and photo-duplicated without restriction, some mention of the original source and contact informing the producer of this modification of their materials is requested.

To conclude, being associated with Project LOEX, and at the center of knowledge of the flurry of activity and enthusiasm in bibliographic instruction today, is a very exciting and interesting position. LOEX would like to thank you, again, for your support and cooperation, and assure all of you that our office will continue to provide as efficient and valuable a service to all librarians in the orientation/instruction arena as we possibly can.

TEACHER/LEARNING INVOLVEMENTS:
WHERE TO FROM HERE?

A.P. Marshall
Dean of Academic Services
Eastern Michigan University

There are no major victories to report in library instructional programs. But there are many instances of significant progress. Over the past twenty five years the library profession has become an aggressive leader in the educational arena. Those years have seen several splinter movements, all of which have in some way been designed to open the portals of rich resources to those who would benefit. Library instruction is only one of such movements.

Perhaps one impetus to this new leadership role assumed by librarians has resulted from the kind of people entering the profession. As our society was recognizing that all people have dreams and aspirations worthy of attention, and that in the struggle for accomplishing those objectives they needed to be equipped to contribute significantly to those around them, librarians emerged as leaders in this movement. We now have come closer to admitting that from the least of our societal members might emerge shapers of a new culture. We now know that being born into a prominent family is no guarantee of continued eminence. From the hovels of Chicago's Southside, St. Louis' Pruitt Igoes, New York's and New Jersey's Stuyvesant neighborhoods, or the Watts communities of the West there may just emerge shakers of our tradition and shapers of our destinies. Malcom X was one who emerged from a path of crime to become a philosophical leader. Martin Luther King was of humble parentage, growing up in the streets of Atlanta, but emerged as a shaker of this country's traditions. Many of today's librarians tell of impoverished beginnings from which they emerged to lead the way in improving the lot of others who without such help might be discouraged from the development of their talents.

Yes, the library profession has accepted the challenges of leadership. No longer are we satisfied to operate in the shadows of our colleagues, the classroom teachers, who may themselves be marked with intellectual impoverishments. It is our newly assumed role to show them that if they remain in the teaching profession, they must give an accounting of their own teaching/learning process. Ours is a great responsibility – that of pointing out that the truly educated men and women of our day must first drink deeply of the "Pierian spring." The empty platitudinal statements about the library being the center of learning on campuses are being pointed out by librarians as being hypocritical. But we are doing it subtly, as we lead both students and faculty to realize the rich educational resources provided by educational-minded librarians.

To illustrate this point, let me provide you with just a few examples of the kinds of programs being envisioned by librarians who are concerned that the library's role in the educational process be recognized.

1. At East Texas State University the librarians have started a program designed "to find a place within the personal teaching methods of individual faculty members where the library and its resources can make a contribution to the learning process," and then "to enhance and modify existing library services from the information gained."

2. The University of Redlands (California) has come to recognize that freshman tours, specialized tours to discuss specific resources available, and working with student interns have "only been a further step along the trail," and "have only scratched the surface." They are now concerned with involving the library and its rich book and human resources in the teaching/learning process by working closely with faculty.

3. Talladega College (Alabama) has recognized that the program of the library could be enhanced if the librarians are allowed "to become involved in planning for curricular developments that would bring about improvements in the total educational process."

4. The Presbyterian College (South Carolina) librarian writes that "the library shares the educational objectives of the faculty, and seeks to support and enrich the entire academic program through aggressive and imaginative integregation of library resources and course work."

5. Wilson College (Pennsylvania) proposes to study the "positive values of using executives of the library to implement library service projects," to study "the benefits to the professor, the students and the librarian of direct classroom association," and to determine "the advantages of using students with special preparation to work with other students."

6. Earlham College has already embarked upon a program of convincing teachers that their objectives can be better met if the rich personal and material resources of the library are properly relied upon.

7. At Lawrence University teachers are learning to rely upon

the expertise of librarians as they make course outlines and daily lesson plans.

These are only seven examples of innovative thinking now going on in libraries across the country. No longer are librarians willing to wait for faculty to realize the importance of library resources in instruction, but they are forging ahead, in some cases coercing teachers into recognizing that their students are being short-changed without library and librarian involvement.

When we speak about involvement in the teaching/learning process, we begin to think about the library's role in the student's education. We are recognizing the value of knowing library resources as an aid to total educational development. The student who understands how to go about finding answers to his own queries is apt to make better grades. This leads to an expansion of the teacher's knowledge by enriching the information imparted in the lecture. This ability to explore on one's own is an enriching experience for a student, and may lead him to acquire much more knowledge than can be achieved by merely listening in class and then reading only the class assignments.

Just how do we propose to improve the teaching/learning experience? First, we must recognize that learning is a process of exploration. To limit a student to the knowledge of the professor is cheating. Yet, some students, particularly from high schools where opportunities for such broadening experiences were not available, have not been properly introduced to the world of knowledge. Often they are afraid that revealing their shortcomings will hold them up to ridicule. So they must be brought subtly to the recognition of the importance of library resources.

The specifics of how librarians become more involved in the teaching/learning process must be determined by the individual situation. As a first step there is a need to understand teaching philosophies as well as teaching methods. Specific interests of the teacher are also important. Once this knowledge is gained, the librarian is ready to proceed further. A simple procedure is to get the faculty member to plan library assignments after consulting with the librarian. This allows the librarian to know what is being assigned so that ample preparations may be made. Sometimes the teacher might invite the librarian to speak to the class on how to locate information on the subject. Many librarians have developed Study Guides, sometimes called Pathfinders or Search Strategies, which are designed to lead the student through several steps to find articles, chapters, books and even audio-visual materials on the subject. Some librarians choose to provide oral instructions while following each student individually. Whichever method is chosen depends on the particular situation.

These activities on the part of your colleagues are changing long held images of librarians. Long seen as second-class citizens in the educational arenas, we are emerging as educational and innovative leaders. Our educational attainments are so often equal or superior that we no longer apologize. We are no less concerned about the educational process, so why should we wait to be led by people who have no more abilities than we?

Future conferences such as this must point the way to a higher level of involvement. If we are to assist students of English as they seek our information on the Romantic Poets, we must not be afraid to let it be known that we know and understand that movement. Better yet, we must not hesitate to guide students and faculty to the literary criticisms which will enhance their appreciations.

Conducting library tours is passé. It really accomplishes little insofar as students are concerned. Teaching courses in library science is too impractical for it can hardly enable us to reach all students. Instructing in a vacuum is useless. There have been enough experimentation in teacher/learning involvement that we know this deserves attention. If our goals of educated college students and graduates are to be realized, we must have input into that operation which directs the students' learning. How it is done is only limited by your own imagination.

COURSE-RELATED LIBRARY INSTRUCTION
IN THE 70's

Thomas Kirk
Science Librarian
Earlham College

"You ask me for something original
I scarcely know where to begin,
For I possess nothing original,
Excepting original sin" (Branscomb, 1940).

Even that is not original for it is the statement of Harvie Branscomb in his introduction to *Teaching with books: a study of college libraries*, which was published in 1940. But it brings me to the theme of my talk today: nothing I have to say is terribly original and yet if the recommendations which I give later were carried out on a wide scale, we would have one of the greatest revolutions in academic library use we have ever seen.

The areas which I intend to cover in today's talk include: (1) the history of the idea of course-related library instruction in the United States; (2) major points about which there is now current agreement; and (3) librarians as an agent of educational change.

I must say parenthetically that I have drawn heavily on the work of two sources: J.E. Scrivener's article in the *Australian Academic and Research Libraries*, and George Bonn's review *Training Laymen in Use of the Library*. I have not cited these two works each time I used them except where I have quoted.

Definition

Before I begin the history of course-related library instruction I want to give you a definition of the term course-related library instruction. It is instruction in the use of *a* library and *the* literature, in relation to an academic program, be it a single course, or a discipline. The instruction is given in the context of a subject and in relation to a specific assignment. This form of instruction is based on the fundamental premise that, as A.G. Neil wrote, "Library skills are, of course, no more than a means to an end and any attempt to

35

elevate them into a study worth pursuing for its own sake is bound to meet with disbelief. If they [library skills] can be communicated by linking them with other studies then their supporting role can be brought out..." (Neil, 1971).

Note when I gave the definition I said nothing about integrated instruction, a phrase which Patricia Knapp (1968), James Kennedy (1970), and others have used. I see integrated instruction as an advanced form of course-related instruction, and I will have more to say about it later. I would also like to point out that I am *not* including the library-college concept in this definition. I have excluded it because of the lack of clarity about the concept, particularly as evidenced by the wide variety of practices that are labeled as examples.

History

George S. Bonn (1960) in his *Training Laymen in Use of the Library*, provides an excellent review of the early history of library instruction. I will not review that history here. However there is a significant issue which I want to discuss. Before 1950 it appears to me that while many librarians and other academicians were concerned about library use and its relationship to course work, there was little attention paid to instructing students in library use. For example in the pre-World War II study of library use that resulted in *Teaching with Books*, Branscomb talks almost exclusively about circulation per student and such issues as whether library reading can be stimulated by professors. The following quotation is a fairly typical example of Branscomb's concerns.

> "Can one get college students to read extensively?
> The answer to this question is not in theoretical but
> in factual terms. Although the average number of
> loans to students has been seen to be depressingly low
> when the calculation is made on a sufficiently large
> basis, there are a number of institutions which have
> demonstrated that under certain conditions under-
> graduates will read much more heavily."

I asked myself why Branscomb, and others of his time who were so concerned about increased use of academic libraries and stimulation of use, did not consider library instruction? We know from other sources (e.g. Columbia University, *President's Annual Report*, 1883, and Peyton Hurt's study: *The Need of College and University Instruction in the Use of the Library*, 1934) that library instruction was an idea which was taken quite seriously by some. I attribute the lack of wide concern to two factors: (1) the nature of under-graduate education, and (2) the size and complexity of college and university libraries. Undergraduate liberal arts education before World War II was classical in nature. Heavy emphasis was placed on the mastery of certain basic information and on the reading of a selected list of "great books." The idea that students might select their own sources to create a researched paper was not yet around. When students did use the library it was far less complex than to-day's academic libraries. There was more emphasis on book collec-tions as opposed to serials, and the number and variety of reference tools found in libraries was considerably less than it is today.

After World War II we begin to see a change both in ideas about the curriculum of undergraduate education and about the need for instruction. So, in 1946, when the College and University Postwar Planning Committee of ALA and ACRL made its recommendations for future actions in which libraries should engage, the committee said, in suggesting that some resources be shifted from acquisitions and cataloging to making better use of the collection:

> "One way that this could be effectively done would
> be through the employment of a teacher-librarian
> or librarians, not giving a separate course in 'library
> instruction,' but cooperating with the instructional
> staff and using classroom assignments as a basis for
> instruction" (Carlson, 1946).

I find it interesting that in this "official" call to action, course-related instruction is specifically mentioned. I suspect, as planning groups generally go, the writers were dreaming a little.

I would now like to turn to developments of the last fifteen years, the period 1960-1975, since George Bonn's 1960 review. The first, and perhaps most important development has been the accelera-tion in the rate of change in undergraduate curricula. Independent study, honors programs, and undergraduate research all with origins earlier in the century have come to have an essential place in much of undergraduate education. These methods have significant implica-tions for libraries and library use, for they make the need for library use more immediate and obvious.

No longer is it enough to worry only about a better relationship between faculty and librarians, and about getting students to use the library more. Now the issue is how to prepare students to make effective and efficient use of the library when their assignments call for it. During the 1960's many institutions responded to that need with "stop gap" approaches. Progress during the period came primar-ily from copying successful programs.

In this development of course-related library instruction during the last 15 years two institutions have made significant contributions through their example. The first of these is Monteith College and Patricia Knapp's library project. It is that project which has given us the theoretical underpinnings for much of what currently is done in course-related bibliographic instruction programs. Perhaps the most famous quote in bibliographic instruction today is Patricia Knapp's summary statement:

> "We conceive of the library as a highly complicated system, or better, a network of interrelated systems, which organizes and controls all kinds of communication." (Knapp, 1966).

In that statement are the roots for such developments as: (1) the demise of the guided tour and (2) the idea of teaching search strategy as well as specific tools. I don't mean to imply by that last statement that the demise of the guided tour and the idea of teaching search strategy began with the Monteith Project – certainly the guided tour and one-hour introduction to the library lecture were on their way out earlier. It is the Monteith Project, in the mid 1960's, that signals the end of an era.

The Monteith Project is also responsible for, as I mentioned earlier, going beyond simple course-related instruction to course-integrated instruction. It was Patricia Knapp's contention that faculty and library staff *together* should design course content, and library assignments, in such a way as to intertwine the two and therefore show how the study of the discipline or subject relates to its literature and its use.

Unfortunately the Monteith Project does *not* provide a workable model for integrated instruction. Or more properly I should say that the dynamics of the Monteith College situation prevented the project from being sustainable. There were probably many factors which attributed to its termination, some of which were beyond the library's control.

The second institution to make a significant contribution has been Earlham College. I say that with a certain timidity since I work at Earlham and am also an Earlham graduate. But bias aside, I still feel that Earlham has made a significant contribution. I suggest that the Earlham program provides that practical workable model which the Monteith Project did not. Earlham's program began some thirteen years ago, and during that time has been sustained, revised, and refined (Farber, 1974). Because of the tremendous interest in library instruction which has coincided with the development of Earlham's program, many ideas which we have had and practices we have tried have been adopted or modified by others.

The tremendous recent increase in interest in library instruction in general has manifested itself in the formation of three national committees within ALA and ACRL and Project LOEX of which you have already heard. We are now seeing the development of a number of state and regional committees and clearinghouses. These organizations are serving three vital functions:

(1) They are collecting information on programs that are in operation.

(2) They are providing local conference programs which are more accessible to staff librarians.

(3) They are promoting the discussion of the pedagogical issues related in library instructions.

However, if these local organizations are to promote the advance of library instruction their activities must be carefully coordinated with that of other local groups and the national groups.

A further manifestation of the depth of the commitment, at least in some segments of the profession, is exemplified by the growing number of advertisements for public service and reference librarians which include library instruction in the job description. I am willing to say that at this time academic librarianship in the United States is on the verge of accepting library instruction as an integral part of the reference services of academic libraries. I will even stick my neck out and predict that this recognition will be firmly established within the profession during the next ten years. This is not to say that the entire profession is committed or will ever be. But I am suggesting that the thrust of current thought is in that direction. This coincides with the increased demand for accountability in the expenditure of funds for libraries, and with the faculty-status-for-librarians movement.

Along with the tremendous interest in library instruction and the growth in the number of programs, there has been an increasing level of agreement on course-related library instruction issues. And where there is no agreement, the discussion has been sufficiently narrowed and the differences more clearly drawn so that evaluation or programs in the decade ahead can contribute to a further significant increase in our ability to provide appropriate library instruction.

The Arising Consensus

I would like to sketch the major points of agreement that are now present in course-related bibliographic instruction. I am only outlining them because there is not time enough to develop each fully and because they have been discussed extensively in the literature (Boner, 1975; Rader, 1975; Lubans, 1974). If there are questions, we can discuss them later. I have listed five areas of agreement: (1) content, (2) teaching methods, (3) objectives, (4) staff, and (5) miscellaneous.

Content

It is now generally agreed that instruction must include (1) orientation, (2) instruction in the use of the library, and (3) instruction in bibliography. Furthermore, the instruction should include both use of specific reference tools and search strategy; they go hand-in-hand.

Teaching Methods

The most effective instruction, according to current wisdom, occurs when a combination of live presentation and some type of follow-up, exercise, or interview, is used. (Parenthetically I should say that media, by and large, is being used as a supplement to, but not a substitute for, live presentations where course-related instruction programs exist.)

Objectives

The need for objectives as the foundation of an instructional program is of recent origin, and originates from the efforts of the ACRL Bibliographic Task Force.

While there certainly is no consensus about the precise objectives which a program should be trying to achieve there are some general areas of agreement. Perhaps most important, an instruction program must change attitudes as well as give factual information. A program should address itself to the poor image of libraries and librarians which students have, and to the misconceptions about how easy academic libraries are to use.

As I said earlier in talking about content, objectives of instruction should include not only the use of a particular library and its collection, but also the bibliography of the student's major subject area. Furthermore, a program of instruction should develop in the student a sensitive balance between independence and dependence in using a reference librarian. Students should be able to interpret their own needs and ask questions in ways which the library can answer. In addition they should have the judgment to know when they have exhausted their expertise and should feel free to ask for help.

Staff

There is now general agreement that the reference staff of a library is a key element in developing a program. Without their support, cooperation, and involvement, a program will not be sustained. They are crucial because of their knowledge of what type of help students need, and, because of their position, are in the ideal place to monitor the results of instruction and act as a feedback mechanism when programs are revised.

But we must face the fact that all reference librarians are not appropriate people to do instruction. It is important to recognize the personal characteristics and qualifications which a librarian must have to be good at instruction: a warm, friendly, non-threatening personality, poise, and the ability to lecture effectively.

Miscellaneous

These last points should not be labeled "miscellaneous" in the sense that they are off-beat and do not fit into any other category. Rather, they are perhaps the most important because they are all pervasive in course-related instruction and are in a sense givens among those involved in course-related instruction today. These points are:

(1) Instruction should only be given when course work requires library use and the instruction when given should prepare the students to do the immediate assignment. Another way of saying this is that instruction should be given when students are ready for it, and it should be directed at what is most important to them -- good grades on the assignments at hand.

(2) Learning to use the library is a continual process, therefore an instruction program should be designed to move students along to different, increasingly sophisticated, levels of library use proficiency.

Librarians as an Agent of Educational Change:
Challenge for the Rest of this Century and Beyond.

To summarize briefly what I have said so far, course-related instruction has been mentioned occasionally in the literature since the late 1800's. However, when the best minds in academia talked about the library as the heart of the college or about ways to integrate the library into the educational program, little mention was made of library instruction. A few early course-related instruction programs did exist at such places as Columbia University Teachers College, the University of Illinois Chicago Undergraduate Division, and Stephens College to name just three. After 1960, programs at Monteith College, Earlham College, and a host of other institutions have propelled course-related library instruction into the forefront of expanding reference services in academic libraries. With this increased interest has come a refined understanding of the nature of instruction and with it, the beginnings of a *modus operandi*; we now have the wherewithal to respond to immediate student needs.

However, if we remain satisfied with that situation, we are admitting satisfaction with Jesse Shera's statement:

> "A librarian, though admittedly a part, and a very
> important part, of the total educational system, is not
> a teacher – at least, he is not a teacher within the formal
> definition of the term. When he acts as a librarian, he
> does not meet classes, he is responsible for no segment
> of the formal curriculum, and he can exercise no
> control over the intellectual progress (or lack of it)
> that the students may experience. (Shera, 1955).

I assert that Shera's statement, especially the last phrase, "... and he can exercise no control over the intellectual progress that the students may experience," is an assumption which we should challenge and a situation we should change. Librarians should assume some responsibility for the education of students. We, as professionals trained in the science and art of bibliography and library use, have a special responsibility to work toward the acceptance of the idea that undergraduate education should, as former Earlham reference librarian Bonnie Frick states, "aim at developing intelligent persons who, independently, can locate and assess the sources of information needed for a wide variety of intellectual, social and personal concerns." (Frick, 1975).

We should not wait for other faculty to put forward this idea, instead we should be pushing it as *one* of the essential tasks of undergraduate education. In my more radical moments I suggest that libraries and librarians should be evaluated, on the basis of how well the institution's students can locate and assess sources of information. For example, what would happen if tenure for librarians was, in part, based on the quality of the library instruction program.

To achieve the goal of institutional recognition that effective and efficient library use is one of the purposes of undergraduate education, librarians must be willing to join the rest of the faculty and administration in the continuing debate within the institution about its purposes and educational goals. But it takes more than

42

just rhetoric; librarians must be ready to work in the trenches. I would therefore offer two caveats:

(1) The library unit as a whole must take a firm and demonstrable position in support of this ideal.

(2) The staff must present themselves as educators willing to work with subject teaching faculty, both on the subject teaching faculty's problems and concerns and on the librarian's.

And remember you are not going to be successful overnight, and maybe never. Keep in mind that there are many obstacles to change – political realities, old attitudes, and the newest, retrenchment. But perhaps the biggest obstacle is our own unwillingness to remain engaged. It is too easy when we become discouraged to withdraw behind our routines and furniture to the peaceful life as an observor.

Conclusion

To close in the view with which I started I would like to offer the following quotation:

> "First, I do not think it is possible to build a good course in any of the areas of human knowledge without a direct relationship between the teacher and the librarian."

> "Secondly, ... I say, that the librarian should serve practically as one of those counselors and friends of the young, who, as soon as the student comes into relationship with books, serves with the teacher to help the student to find his way through reading lists, and to utilize the various modes of learning possible through books."

> "Thirdly, ... for the typical course in literature, philosophy, psychology, or in those areas of humanities where teachers are trying to experiment with new kinds of courses which interrelate one discipline with another, ... the librarian has ... a direct role to play in the planning of the courses themselves." (Taylor, 1954).

These are *not* the words of a library instruction librarian speaking in 1976. No, they are the words of the former President of Sarah Lawrence College, Henry Taylor, speaking to academic librarians in 1954. Will a speaker at some future library conference repeat my opening lines,

> "You ask me for something original
> I scarcely know where to begin,
> For I possess nothing original?"

The fruits of your efforts will provide the answer.

BIBLIOGRAPHY

Annual Report of the President. New York: Columbia University, 1883.

Bonn, George S. "Training in the Use of the Library." *The State of the Library Art,* edited by Ralph R. Shaw, vol. 2, part 1. New Brunswick, N.J.: Rutgers University, Graduate School of Library Service, 1960.

Bolner, Mary. *Planning and Developing a Library Orientation Program.* Proceedings of the Third Annual Conference on Libraries, Eastern Michigan University. Ann Arbor: Pierian Press, 1975.

Branscomb, Harvie. *Teaching with Books: a Study of College Libraries.* Chicago: American Library Association, 1940.

Carlson, William H. *College and University Libraries and Librarianship; an Examination of their Present Status and Some Proposals for their Future Development.* Prepared by the College and University Postwar Planning Committee of American Library Association and the Association of College and Reference Libraries. Chicago: American Library Association, 1946.

Farber, Evan Ira. "Library Instruction Throughout the Curriculum: Earlham College Program." In, *Educating the Library User,* edited by John Lubans, pp. 145-162. New York: Bowker, 1974.

Frick, Elizabeth. "Information Structure and Bibliographic Instruction." *Journal of Academic Librarianship* (1975): 12-14.

Hurt, Peyton. "The Need of College and University Instruction in Use of the Library." *Library Quarterly* (1934): 436-448.

Kennedy, James R. "Integrated Library Instruction." *Library Journal* 95 (1970): 1450-1453.

Knapp, Patricia. *The Monteith College Library Experiment.* New York: Scarecrow Press, 1966.

Lubans, John. *Educating the Library User.* New York: Bowker, 1975.

Neil, A.G. "Library Tutoring." *Education Libraries Bulletin* no. 42 (1971): 9-12.

Rader, Hannelore B. *Academic Library Instruction, Objectives, Programs, and Faculty Involvement*. Papers of the Fourth Annual Conference on Library Orientation for Academic Libraries, Eastern Michigan University. Ann Arbor: Pierian Press, 1975.

Scrivener, J.E. "Instruction in Library Use: the Persisting Problem." *Australian Academic and Research Libraries* (1972):87-119.

Shera, Jesse H. *The Role of the College Library -- a Reappraisal in Library-Instructional Integration on the College Level*. Report of the 40th Conference of Eastern College Librarians. (ACRL Monographs 13) Chicago: Association of College and Reference Librarians, pp. 6-13.

Taylor, Harold *The Role of the College Library - a Reappraisal in Library-Instructional Integration on the College Level*. Report of the 40th Conference of Eastern college Librarians. (ACRL Monograph 13) Chicago: Association of College and Reference Librarians, pp. 13-16.

LIBRARY-USE INSTRUCTION IN
MIDDLE EAST ACADEMIC LIBRARIES
and
THE LIBRARY EXPERIENCE:
A CROSS-CULTURAL ANALYSIS

Richard H. Dewey
University Librarian
American University in Cairo

Library-use instruction is a fairly new phenomena in the academic libraries of the Middle East. This presentation is a report on the state of the art, with a comparative analysis of students in Montreal and Cairo. It will, of necessity, speak in broad, general terms.

The Middle East falls in the category of "developing countries." Some are more developed than others. Using Western standards – if that is a measurement – some of the countries, aspects of them, are well into the twentieth century, while others are just coming out of the eighteenth.

There are enormous cultural, political and economic differences among these twenty six nations of the Middle East. At times it seems there are twenty six national solutions. Differences aside, Middle Eastern leaders look upon the printed word as the major vehicle of communication.

Veneration of the work or book has a long tradition in the Middle East. We know that much of what has been passed on to us is the basis of our Western civilization. The libraries of the mosque, the church, the synagogue, have throughout history preserved the book.

National and university libraries were established in most of the countries in the twentieth century. In some countries, the colonial powers encouraged this establishment. Library schools and training programs have been set up in a few of the nations.

These libraries, along with the countries, are still "developing." One never knows what to expect when visiting a library. Chaos seems to reign in some, while in others one can see that the librarian in charge is capable of managing a library anywhere in the world. We specifically mention the librarian. He or she seems to be vital factor in the libraries visited.

There are major problems to consider as they affect the establishment of a library-use instruction program. Before we enter the library, one extremely important area concerns the educational system.

Today, we are often critical of the various educational systems. In the West it is almost fashionable to criticize; any number of experiments and systems have been tried and are being tried. One does not have that impression in the Middle East. The teaching methods generally do not encourage students to use a library or develop the need to search for materials in research. Until students are well into advanced graduate research, independent work is just not in the picture. Lectures and examinations encourage the students to memorize. The experienced librarian knows that the library will serve as no more than a study hall if students need only prepare for examinations.

Once the student enters the library, he or she is faced with three major obstacles: inadequate bibliographical sources, closed stacks and poorly trained reference staff.

The bibliographical sources are undoubtedly the major obstacle. There are two tools taken for granted in libraries in the West which are largely unavailable in the Middle East: the card catalog and periodical indexes/abstract services.

In many academic libraries there is only one approach to finding out which books are available and that is through the main entry. If you know your author, there is some sort of index available.

Reference sources in Arabic, Hebrew, Persian and Turkish are sorely lacking. Librarians are deeply concerned with filling this gap and are working to produce them. For the moment there is heavy reliance on Western titles.

There are indexes for periodicals published in the national languages in Iran, Israel and Turkey. One published in Cairo in the mid-1960's that indexed periodicals in Arabic in Egypt has ceased publication. Another approach has been through publishing a bibliographical supplement to a journal that lists publications about the country. There is one very good Tunisian journal that lists all social science publications concerning Tunisia.

English and French play a major role in the educational systems. The sciences are taught exclusively in one of these two languages in a number of Middle Eastern countries. Scientific journals are also published in English and French, in addition to a handful of indexes and abstract services covering these journals.

The libraries often have more Western language periodicals than those which are published locally; this is particularly true in the sciences and social sciences. However, the accompanying indexes are not available in most of the libraries, which often cannot afford these expansive services, nor is the reference staff always aware they exist. Inquiries in a few libraries as to why there were no indexes in the reference room lead to the response that teachers and students do not ask for them! (The author had a similar experience in Paris ten years ago).

Closed stacks are a second obstacle that students face when they enter the library. Faculty usually have the privilege of entering the stacks. There are exceptions: new libraries in Jordan, Israel and Libya have open stacks. American influence as regards open access is evident in the American universities in Beirut and Cairo; Bogazicci in Istanbul (formerly Roberts College); Middle East Technical University of Petroleum and Minerals in Dhahran, Saudi Arabia. The British left behind an open stack library in Khartoum. University research institute libraries usually have open access.

The third obstacle concerns personnel. Library science faces a major problem in the Middle East. One simply cannot attract the better students. Tradition and societal pressure push the best into engineering, medicine and law. In a part of the world where status plays a most important role, librarians are still viewed as guardians of the books. Hence the librarian is not effective in the educational system. This factor has greatly hindered establishment of library-use instruction programs.

We know that there is a desperate need to train students in the proper use of the library. Graduate students use a traditional approach when searching for bibliographic sources. It is traditional in that the student is still directed to specific publications by their professors. At the American University of Beirut and the American University in Cairo, we have seen hundreds of students from national universities who have only the vaguest idea of how to use the card catalog. They not only need to have every reference source explained, but often want the reference librarian to produce the materials. The same can be said of a visiting professor or researcher.

There is a general concern for improvement in reference services, including library-use instruction. The subject appears in the literature produced in the Middle East and it also comes up in conversation with head librarians. Foreign librarians who have worked in the libraries have also discussed it in articles. Library-use instruction has been included in national meetings, and in the case of the Arab countries, international meetings. (Arab Universities Union: Cairo, 1970; Damascus, 1971; Baghdad, 1972; UNESCO, Cairo 1974.)

In order to learn what is being done in the university libraries, fifty-five questionnaires were sent to the Arab countries, Iran, Israel and Turkey. Thirty were returned.

QUESTIONNAIRE AND RESULTS

1. Number of professionally trained librarians. The answers varied enormously. The question was possibly misunderstood in several cases: meaning the total number of staff. However, "professionally trained" in some countries, means two years following high school.

2. Are students taken on a tour of the library? — yes 27 no 3

3. Is there a program to teach students how to use a library? — yes 19 no 11

4. If there is a program it began approximately which year?

1940's	1
1950's	1
1960's	5
1970's	9
1976	3

5. If there is a program are all students required to participate? — yes 4 no 15

6. If there is a program, how many librarians are involved?

Programs	Librarians
11	1
4	2
1	3
1	5
1	6
1	No ans.

7. Do librarians participate in bibliographical instruction in the classroom? — yes 12 no 6 / no answer 12

8. Is bibliographic instruction or lessons on how to use a library taught by the classroom teacher? — yes 17 no 13

9. Is there a faculty or department of library science in the university? — yes 13 no 17

50

INDIVIDUAL RESPONSES TO QUESTIONNAIRE

	1.	2.	3.	4.	5.	6.	7.	8.	9.
American Univ. in Cairo	12	yes	yes	1960s	no	1	yes	no	yes
American Univ. of Beirut	12	yes	yes	1960s	yes	1	no	yes	no
Beirut Univ. College	1	yes	yes	1950s	no	1	yes	no	yes
Ben Gurion Univ. Beersheba	?	yes	yes	1970	no	1	yes	yes	no
Benghazi Univ.	5	yes	no	–	–	–	–	no	no
Beth Gordon Institute Israel	1	yes	yes	1941	no	2	no	no	no
Bogazici Univ. Istanbul	6	yes	yes	1960	yes	6	yes	yes	no
Cairo Univ.	25	yes	yes	1975	no	1	yes	yes	yes
Gulf Technical College, Baherein	2	yes	no	–	–	–	–	no	no
Hacettepe Univ. Ankara	18	yes	yes	1967	no	2	yes	yes	yes
Hebrew Univ. Jerusalem	120	yes	yes	1961	no	2	yes	yes	yes
Istanbul Univ.	6	yes	no	–	–	–	–	no	yes
Kuwait Univ.	20	yes	no	–	–	–	–	no	no
Lebanese Univ. Science Library	2	yes	yes	1976	no	1	no	no	no

Middle East Technical Univ. Ankara	21	yes	yes	1970s	yes	1	no	no	no
Mustansiriyah Univ., Baghdad	20	no	no	–	–	–	–	yes	yes
Pahlavi Univ. Shiraz	6	yes	yes	1976	no	1	no	yes	yes
Riyadh Univ.	40	yes	no	–	–	–	–	yes	yes
Tashreen Univ. Latakiya	1	no	no	–	–	–	–	no	no
Tehran Univ.	6	yes	no	–	–	–	–	yes	yes
Tehran Univ. Faculty of Veterinary Medicine	10	yes	yes	1976	yes	–	yes	yes	yes
Tel Aviv Univ.	80	yes	yes	1972	no	1	no	yes	no
Tel Hai Regional College Israel	1	yes	yes	1973	no	2	yes	yes	yes
Univ. d'Alger	5	no	no	–	–	–	–	yes	yes
Univ. de Constantine	6	yes	yes	1970s	no	3	yes	no	no
Univ. of Haifa	59	yes	yes	1971	no	1	yes	yes	yes
Univ. of Jordan	10	yes	no	–	–	–	yes	yes	no
Univ. of Khartoum	7	yes	no	–	–	–	–	no	no
Univ. of Khartoum Centre for African & Asian Studies	1	yes	yes	1975	no	1	yes	yes	no
Univ. of Petroleum & Minerals, Dharan	33	yes	yes	1975	no	5	no	no	no

Was there any relationship between having a library school in the university and having a library-use instruction program? The answers would seem to indicate that the presence of a library school has little influence.

There is a program and a library school	8
There is a program and no library school	11
There is no program and there is a library school	5
There is no program and there is no library school	6
	30

The library school's presence appears to have no effect on required attendance when there is a program. Some of the responses gave one the impression that the repondents did not fully understand the meaning of a program in library-use instruction.

What methods are used to teach students library use? There is a standard tour. When lectures are offered, it is probably the tried method of gathering a few references together, i.e., the passive approach. Several libraries sent standard library handbooks, some of which state that there is a program offered. The University of Petroleum and Minerals handbook describes a program offered over a three year period, each increasing in sophistication. This is a new program; it will be interesting to learn how it succeeds. Eleven of the universities requested copies of materials that are used in the American University in Cairo. The university of Haifa, the American University of Beirut and Cairo University reported that they use audio-visual materials.

The library was integrated into a research methodology course at Kuwait University in 1974. When it was proposed to set up a required program, they faced the familiar problem of initial rejection by the University Faculty Council. There is a course at Cairo University which reaches several hundred first-year students.

This is a general picture of the state of the art in the Middle East academic libraries. Let us now move on to the second part of the report: a comparison of students in Montreal and Cairo.

THE LIBRARY EXPERIENCE: A COMPARATIVE STUDY

The Library Experience was originally designed in 1971. We were concerned with reaching large numbers of students. The repetitive lecture is time-consuming and difficult to evaluate. Audio-visual programs, while useful as a supplement, are basically passive. There were programs that attempted to create "little librarians;" while others taught use of the library in a vacuum.

The Library Experience was therefore designed:

1. to be active, not passive.
2. to teach first year students the basic reference sources which all university students should know, and how to use them.
3. to teach advanced students the bibliographical sources in the major fields.
4. to require each student to complete it in terms of the individual's research topic.
5. to avoid allowing students to give the identical answer to all of the questions in a standard library exercise.
6. to take the students methodically through each of the reference sources, as a reference librarian would recommend.
7. to require students to approach the reference librarian.
8. to permit a minimum of time to correct each Experience.

The Library Experience was first used at Sir George Williams University, Montreal, an urban setting with 6,000 full-time and 6,000 part-time students. The Experience went through several "editions" as we collected enough data to analyze its use for new groups of students.

It was next used at the American University in Cairo, also in an urban setting; a small, private, liberal arts school, with 1500 students, ninety percent of whom are Egyptian.

The students, while from different countries and cultures, had one thing in common: they had a similar experience with libraries or lack thereof in both countries. Public and school libraries in Montreal are sorely lacking. Students in numerous classes were asked how many had ever been in a library: the answer was usually two or three out of a group of twenty-two students. Public and school libraries are a very new phenomena in Cairo; there was no need to pose the question.

The program is basically the same in both institutions. The students are taken on a tour of the library. A tour quiz is administered in the classroom. It is sent to the Orientation Librarian for corrections and returned. When the teacher informs the Orientation Librarian that the students are going to start searching for materials for the term paper, then and only then, do students use the Library Experience. The Experiences are corrected in the library and returned to the students.

Data was collected on Library Experiences completed by 75 students on each of the universities. The following table lists the results.

LIBRARY EXPERIENCE*
COMPARATIVE USE BY 150 STUDENTS IN THE AMERICAN UNIVERSITY IN CAIRO (AUC) AND SIR GEORGE WILLIAMS UNIVERSITY, MONTREAL (SGWU)

	AUC	SGWU
1. Encyclopedia		
Appropriate subject heading from the index volume	72	70
2. Card Catalog		
Subject section		
a. Completed	72	73
b. Subject heading related to topic	72	72
c. Titles in place of subject headings	4	2
d. Subject headings are in card catalog	71	72
Author-Title section		
a. Completed	71	69
b. Book of essays not in the library (correct)	23	17
c. Book of essays not in the library (incorrect)	4	8
3. *Essay and General Literature Index*		
a. Completed	72	70
b. Appropriate subject headings	71	73
c. Totally misunderstood	5	3
4. Periodical indexes		
a. Article published after 1970	71	72
b. Used *Bibliographic Index*	1	0
c. Included title of article	74	72
d. Used abbreviation for title of periodical	2	2
e. Title of index, volume number, pages in place of title of periodical	1	3
f. Periodical not listed in Serials Holdings list (correct)	20	11
g. Periodical not listed in Serials Holdings list (incorrect)	7	3
h. Library does not have volume wanted (correct)	6	5
i. Library does not have volume wanted (incorrect)	3	1
5. Dictionaries – Quotations		
Completed	71	73

6. Dictionaries -- Synonyms and antonyms   71   73

7. Biographies   75   75

8. Bibliographies
   a. Completed   68   66
   b. Subject heading related to topic   69   72
   c. Correct subject heading, but it is not a
      bibliography   13   17

9. Book reviews
   a. Completed   58   65
   b. Totally misunderstood   2   1
   c. Listed periodical title containing book
      review   72   73
   d. Listed title of book rather than title of
      periodical   2   4
   e. Bibliographical information about BRD
      rather than periodical with book review   2   2
   f. Listed volume, date and pages of periodical   7   70

*See Appendix.

What do the results show? Clearly, the Library Experience can be adapted to the small as well as the big university. The students do about the same in both schools. The quality of work is nearly identical and there are about the same number who did not complete the various sections. They seem to have little problem with the subject headings in the catalogs and indexes. In Cairo, they found fewer essays and periodicals, which is due to the size of the collection. Several did not understand the concept of sub-headings, as shown in the search for bibliographies in the catalog.

Incomplete work increases as they near the end of the Experience. They were either too tired to complete the section on book reviews or perhaps did not see the value of looking for one. It may be due to the research topic.

What topics did the students select for the term paper? Out of fifty students in Cairo, nine selected topics in the sciences (two duplications); thirty nine in the social sciences (seven duplications); and three in the humanities. Seven topics dealt specifically with the Middle East.

It is interesting to list just a few of the topics. Research topics included space explorations (two aspects), lasers, energy, the nervous system, population (five aspects), economic development, women, marriage, divorce, patriotism and Islam. Psychology was a popular area: twelve students were researching various aspects of that discipline.

Data was not kept for students in Montreal, but the experienced librarian can see a great similarity in the interests among the students in the two cultures. Are youth interested in the same subjects on an international scale?

Do we know if it works? The results would show that the great majority of the students did well using the Library Experience. Informal discussions with teachers in both institutions are encouraging. They report that the quality of the papers and bibliographies has improved. It also saves the teacher endless numbers of hours. The students work by themselves and with the reference librarian. With a corrected Experience in hand, they have immediate feedback.

LIBRARY EXPERIENCES

1. This is a Library Experience. It is not a test. It involves learning how to use some of the basic search techniques and bibliographical tools that you will need to know in order to begin research on your term paper.

   Some of the reference sources may not pertain directly to your topic. These sources are brought to your attention as basic guides that all University students should know.

2. The answers require complete bibliographic citation. You should purchase *MLA Style Sheet* or *Manual for Writers of Term Papers, Theses and Dissertations* at the University Bookstore. These guide lists have the correct bibliographical citation forms.

3. The A.U.C. Library brochure is available at the various public service desks. It will assist you in locating the various research sources and library services.

4. Several printed handouts are available describing footnotes and bibliographies; dictionaries; the card catalog, etc.

5. Unless otherwise indicated, the sources you will use are located in the *Reference Room*, second floor.

6. REMEMBER. There is a Reference Librarian available to assist you everyday from 8:00 a.m. to 5:00 p.m.

LIBRARY EXPERIENCE – GENERAL INTRODUCTION

1. Encyclopedia

   Use an encyclopedia for general background reading on a subject. Multi-volume sets usually include an index volume. You should always begin your search for information in the *index*.

   ENCYCLOPAEDIA BRITANNICA   Ref AE 5 E363

   ENCYCLOPEDIA AMERICANA   Ref AE 5 E333

   WORLD BOOK ENCYCLOPEDIA   Ref AE 5 W55

   دائرة معارف الشعب   Ref DS 37 D3

   Use one of these encyclopedias and look for background material that will assist you in your research topic.

   Title of Encyclopedia used_____

   Subject heading (term) used in the *index* volume?_____
   _____

   The article is in volume number_____

2. Almanacs

There are reference guides published annually that review events or developments during the previous year. They contain a wealth of factual information.

INFORMATION PLEASE ALMANAC   Ref AY 64 I55

WHITAKER'S ALMANAC   Ref AY 754 W5

WORLD ALMANAC   Ref AY 67 N5 W7

UNITED ARAB REPUBLIC ANNUAL
  STATISTICAL HAND BOOK   (Ask at Reference
                                  Desk)

Use one of these almanacs and look for information related to your topic.

Almanac used_____

Year_____

Found on page_____

HOW TO USE THE CARD CATALOGUE

The card catalogue is an alphabetically arranged index to books kept in the library. It is divided into two separate sections: an author-title catalogue and a subject catalogue.

AUTHOR-TITLE CATALOGUE
Consists of cards for all works *by* personal and corporate authors and editors as well as titles.

SUBJECT CATALOGUE
Consists of cards with capitalized subject headings for all works *about* personal and corporate authors, topical subjects and political jurisdictions as subjects.

EXAMPLES
Individuals as Authors

al-Afghani, Jamal al-Din, 1838-1897.

Faulkner, William, 1897-1962.

Hugo, Victor, 1802-1885.

Lawrence, David Herbert, 1885-1900.

Saroyan, William, 1908–

Corporate Bodies as Authors (Includes government bodies, association, firms, political parties, conferences, etc.)

Cairo, Dar al-Kutub al-Misriyah, Qism al-Irshad.

National Council of Teachers of English.

Staatliche Museen Zu Berlin.

EXAMPLES
Individuals as subjects (includes works of these individuals as subjects)

al-Afghani, Jamal al-Din, 1838-1897.

Flaubert, Gustave, 1821-1880. Madame Bovary.

O'Neil, Eugene Gladstone, 1888-1953.

Shakespeare, William -- Bibliography -- Folios.

Corporate Bodies as Subjects (Includes government bodies, associations, firms, institutions, political parties, etc.)

American Telephone and Telegraph Company.

Financial Institutions – U.S. – Addresses, Essays, Lectures.

Massachusetts Institute of Technology.

United Nations Educational,
Scientific and Cultural
Organization.

U.S. Library of Congress.
African Section.

Titles

Political Jurisdictions as Subjects (Works about countries, states, provinces, cities, etc.)

The child's conception of geometry.

Greece -- History.

La divina commedia.

Red Sea -- Description and Geography.

Goethe in Briefen.

Tunisia -- History.

Mawahib al-Jalil.

Les misérables.

For whom the bell tolls.

Topical Subjects

American Prose Literature -- 20th Century -- History and Criticism.

Bibliography -- Best Books -- Fiction.

Europe -- Social Conditions.

Psychology, Pathological.

SUBJECT
HEADING

SEE
ALSO
RELATED
SUBJECT
HEADINGS

```
VM          EGYPT -- ANTIQUITIES
16          Landström, Björn
L3413          Ships of the Pharaohs; 4000 years of Egyptian
1971        ship--building. Drawings by the author  Garden
            City, N.Y., Doubleday, 1971.

                159 p.  illus.

                Bibliography:  p.150--152.

                1. Ship--building -- Egypt.  2. Egypt --
            Antiquities.  I. Title.
```

AUTHOR

```
VM          Landström, Björn
16              Ships of the Pharoahs; 4000 years of Egyptian
L3413       ship--building. Drawings by the author.  Garden
1971        City, N.Y., Doubleday, 1971.

                159 p.  illus.

                Bibliography:  p.150--152.

                1. Ship--building -- Egypt.  2. Egypt --
            Antiquities.  I. Title
```

TITLE

VM   Ships of the Pharaohs; 4000 years of Egyptian
16   ship–building.
L3413 Landström, Björn
1971   Ships of the Pharaohs; 4000 years of Egyptian
ship–building. Drawings by the author. Garden
City, N.Y., Doubleday, 1971.

159 p. illus.

Bibliography: p.150–152.

1. Ship--building – Egypt. 2. Egypt --
Antiquities. I. Titles.

65

3. Card Catalogue

   a) Subject section

   Find the subject headings in the card catalogue that are most appropriate to your research topic. If you have trouble finding the appropriate terminology in the subject catalogue, ask for assistance at the Information Desk. What *subject headings* did you find in the subject card catalogue? List at least two. Do *not* list titles.

SEE SAMPLE _____
CATALOGUE _____
CARDS _____

   b) Author/Title section

   This is to be completed after you do the exercise on the *ESSAY AND GENERAL LITERATURE INDEX* (no. 4).

   Look in this section of the card catalogue for the book that includes the essay you located in *ESSAY AND GENERAL LITERATURE INDEX*. If the library has this book, you will find it listed under the title as well as the author or editor.

   Is the book of essays in the library?_____

   Give the complete bibliographical information:

   Author or editor_____

   Title_____

   Publisher_____

   Place of publication (city)_____

   Date of publication_____

   Number of pages_____

   Call number_____   You will need it to
                                 locate the book on the
                                 shelf in the stacks.

4. Essays

You may not be able to find what you want in the card catalogue or the topic you are researching may be so popular that all of the books on the subject may be already checked out. It is at this point you can turn to essays.

ESSAY AND GENERAL LITERATURE INDEX Ref. AI 3 E752

It is a guide to essays, arranged by subject. If, for example, you are researching a paper on student clubs: find the heading in the *Index* and choose one essay appropriate to your topic.

An example of the information as it appears in the *Index*.

STUDENT CLUBS' SEE STUDENTS' SOCIETIES.

STUDENTS' SOCIETIES
Lozoff, M.M. Residential groups and individual development.
In Katz, J. and associates. No time for youth. p255-317.

Subject heading you used in the *Index*?_____

Year(s) used_____

Author of essay_____

Title of essay_____

Title of book that contains the essay (follows word *In*)
_____

Editor or author of book of essays_____

Page numbers of the essay_____

Now look in the author/title section of the card catalogue to see if the library has this book of essays.

5. Periodical Indexes

These are the indexes to periodicals that you will need to use to find the most current information on a topic. Note that the terms "periodical," "journal," "serial," and "magazine" are used interchangeably.

The indexes are located on the index tables in the Reference Room (second floor).

READERS' GUIDE TO PERIODICAL LITERATURE

SOCIAL SCIENCES AND HUMANITIES INDEX

PUBLIC AFFAIRS INFORMATION SERVICE (P.A.I.S.)

There are also periodical indexes in specific subject areas, for example, *Applied Science and Technology Index, Business Periodicals Index,* etc. Ask the Reference Librarian for the index most appropriate to your research topic. An example of the information as it appears in an index:

YOUTH
  Early marriage: a propositional formulation
  K.W. Bartz and F.I. Nye. bibliog J. Marriage
  and Fam. 32:258-68 My '70

Here's what it means:

Youth – Subject heading

Early marriage: a propositional formulation -- title of article

K.W. Bartz and F.I. Nye -- Authors

Bibliog -- The article includes a bibliography

32 – Volume number

258-68 -- Page numbers

My '70 -- Date – May 1970

Note the use of abbreviations. Abbreviations are used extensively in all library reference books. They are usually listed at the *front* of the index volume.

Use one index and give the complete bibliographical citation for an article appropriate to your research topic. Find an article published *after 1970*.

Title of periodical index used_____

Subject heading used_____

Title of article_____

Title of periodical (complete title, not abbreviation)_____
_____

Volume number_____Pages_____

Date of publication (month and year)_____

Next you will need to find out if the AUC Library has the periodical you want to read. Today there are so many periodicals published that no one library can afford to have all of them.

The *SERIES HOLDINGS LIST* is an alphabetical list of all periodicals and serial publications in the AUC Library. It is located on the public services desks.

An example of an entry in the *SERIES HOLDINGS LIST*:

MIDDLE EAST JOURNAL
1947 -- (INC.)

incomplete

The dash (–) following the year (1947–) indicates that the Library has a continuing subscription.

Is the periodical you want listed in the *SERIALS HOLDINGS LIST*?_____

Does the Library have the volume you want?_____

Is it in the original format?_____or microform?_____

Is it on the shelf?_____

6. Dictionaries

   Dictionaries are the key sources for information about words; their meaning, spelling, pronunciation, usage, synonyms and antonyms.

   a) Dictionaries – General.

   WEBSTER'S THIRD NEW INTERNATIONAL DICTION-ARY Ref. PE 1625 W36

   SHORTER OXFORD ENGLISH DICTIONARY REF. PE 1625 M72

   AL-MAWRID: A Modern English-Arabic Dictionary Ref. PJ 6640 B35 1970

   Use a dictionary and select a word of your choice:

   Dictionary used_____

   Word_____

   Meaning in English_____

   Meaning in Arabic_____

b) Dictionaries – Quotations

You may encounter a famous quotation or know all or part of one and want to know who said it.

OXFORD DICTIONARY OF QUOTATIONS Ref PN 6081 09

BENHAN'S BOOK OF QUOTATIONS Ref PN 6080 B35

THE INTERNATIONAL THESAURUS OF QUOTATIONS Ref PN 6081 T77

Use a dictionary of quotations and select one quotation in a subject of your choice (example: Women, Liberty, Love, Life....)

Subject_____

Quotation_____

_____

_____

Dictionary used_____

_____

Page_____

c) Dictionaries – Synonyms & Antonyms.

General dictionaries include a few synonyms. There are guides that list many more.

ROGET'S INTERNATIONAL THESAURUS Ref PE 1591 M37

ALLENS SYNONYMS AND ANTONYMS Ref PE 1591 A5

Use one of the synonyms dictionaries and look up a word.

Dictionary used_____

A word of your choice_____

Synonyms _____

7. Atlases & Gazetteers

An atlas is a collection of maps. These maps may show many kinds of information besides geographical features, national boundaries and the location of cities. For example, some atlases display information about population distribution, major resources, seas, routes, etc.

A gazetteer is a geographical dictionary which gives the pronunciation and location of place – names, historical and socio-economic information.

TIMES ATLAS Ref G 1019 T5

INTERNATIONAL ATLAS Ref G 1019 R355

WORLD ATLAS Ref G 1019 H501

THE COLUMBIA LIPPINCOTT GAZETTEER OF THE WORLD Ref G 103 L7

THE TIMES INDEX – GAZETTEER OF THE WORLD Ref G 103 T5

Use one of the atlases and look for the population figures of a capital city in Africa, Asia or Europe.

Atlas or Gazetteer used_____

Capital city_____

Population_____Year_____

8. Biographies

Very often you will need to know some facts about a person. There are guides that you may turn to in place of reading a biography or an autobiography.

CURRENT BIOGRAPHY Ref CT 100 C8

20th CENTURY AUTHORS Ref PN 771 K86

WHO'S WHO IN THE ARAB WORLD Ref D198.3 W5

72

Use one of these guides and look up a biography of your choice about an author.

Which biographical guide did you use?_____

Name of author_____

Birth date_____

Place of birth_____

Two of his or her publications_____

```
PR            JOHNSON, SAMUEL, 1709--1784 -- BIBLIOGRAPHY
3533
W3        Wahba, Magdi, ed.
1962          Johnsonian studies, including a
          bibliography of Johnsonian studies, 1950--1960,
          compiled by James L. Clifford and Donald J.
          Greene.  Cairo (Societé orientale de
          publicité)    1962.
              350 p.

              1. Johnson, Samuel, 1709--1784.  2. Johnson,
          Samuel, 1709--1784 -- Bib.  I. Title.
```

```
Ref           ENGLISH LITERATURE -- BIBLIOGRAPHY
Z
2011      Bateson, Frederick Wilse, 1901--
B28           The Cambridge bibliography of English
1940      literature, edited by F.W. Bateson.  Cambridge,
          Eng., The University press, 1940--57.
              5v.
              Contents. -- I. 600--1660 -- II. 1660--1800.--
          III. 1800--1900.  IV. Index -- Supplements:  A.D.
          600--1900, ed. by G. Watson.

              1. English literature -- Bibl.  I. The Cambridge
          history of English literature.  II. Title.
```

GENERAL

74

9. Bibliographies

You will want to know what has already been published on the topic you are researching. These publications are listed in bibliographies. Bibliographies are appended to encyclopedia articles, books, and periodical articles. They are also published as individual books.

Bibliographies are listed in the *subject* card catalogue as a *subheading* of the subject you are searching.

For example:

DRAMA – BIBLIOGRAPHY

KORAN -- BIBLIOGRAPHY

ARAB COUNTRIES -- BIBLIOGRAPHY

EGYPT -- BIBLIOGRAPHY

You will be looking for information on a specific topic. For example, you may want to see a list of publications about *Samuel Johnson*. If the library has a bibliography on *Samuel Johnson* it will appear in the subject card catalog:

JOHNSON, SAMUEL, 1709-1784 -- BIBLIOGRAPHY

SEE SAMPLE
CATALOGUE
CARDS

However, you may have to begin your search using a more general subject heading:

ENGLISH LITERATURE – BIBLIOGRAPHY

Find a bibliography on your research topic.
What subject heading did you find in the card catalogue?
--Bibliography
_____
Author or editor_____
Title_____
Call number_____

75

10. Book Reviews

You might find it useful to read a review of one of the books you are reading in conjunction with your research.

In order to locate a book review that has appeared in periodicals or newspapers you must first have the exact year of publication, author and title. Four indexes that list the periodical in which a book review was published:

BOOK REVIEW INDEX Ref Z 1035 A1 B6

BOOK REVIEW DIGEST Ref Z 1219 C96

INDEX TO BOOK REVIEWS IN THE HUMANITIES Ref Z 1035 A1 I63

LIBRARY JOURNAL BOOK REVIEW Ref Z 1035 A1 L48

Use any of these. Look in the volume for *the year* the book was published. You may need to look in the volume for the following year. If there is a review it is listed under the author's name. The bibliographical information is listed in the same way as in a periodical index.

Look for a book review of one of the books you are reading for your research topic.

Which index did you use?_____Year?_____

List one of the reviews you read:

Title of book_____

Date of publication of the book_____

Periodical title in which the review was published (Complete title; not the abbreviations)_____
_____

Volume number_____

Date of publication (month and year)_____

Page numbers_____

Remember in order to find out if this periodical is in the library, you have to check the *Serials Holdings List*, located on the Reference Desk.

THE STATE OF LIBRARY INSTRUCTION CREDIT COURSES
and the
STATE OF THE USE OF LIBRARY SKILLS WORKBOOKS

Miriam Dudley
Reference Librarian
College Library
University of California, Los Angeles

While it is true that not all librarians recognize the necessity or even the propriety of teaching their users how to use their library, it is certainly not necessary to argue the need for instruction to those attending this Sixth Annual Conference on Library Instruction. As the 60's came to a close, library literature revealed fewer why-we-should articles than how-we-should. Now, in the middle of the first year of the last half of the 70's, it is well established in the minds of most working librarians that college graduates are lamentably uninformed about the nature of and access to the resources of libraries, and many of us are involved in a search for solutions and resolutions to this problem.

Earlham has for a number of years been offering its impressive and successful program in relating library instruction to the curriculum. The more traditional approach, the one most commonly used in academic libraries however, is the accredited academic, formal classroom course. While these courses vary in the number of hours of credit, in the grading, in use of textual materials, in depth, scope and intensity, there is, suprisingly perhaps, little disagreement on the basic body of knowledge to be imparted. All of the courses I've seen or read about require the student to have some knowledge of or experience with the card catalog, government documents, encyclopedias, news and periodical indexes and abstracts, almanacs, atlases, dictionaries, handbooks, biographical and book reviewing sources, microform, and the elements of bibliography; some add, some subtract, some expose students to numerous sources, some to few, some teach research methodology, but basically we are in agreement as to *what* should be taught.

We aren't even in disagreement as to *how* we should teach. Most of us see the necessity for a multi-level, multi-faceted approach. Most of us would like to offer instruction ranging from the basic library tour to the self-paced general course of instruction to the formal classroom course in bibliography to subject-oriented individualized tutoring.

The problem for many libraries is finding an academic home and academic support for these courses. The experience of the libraries of the nine University of California campuses clearly exemplifies some of the problem areas of accredited courses in the 70's, how the matter of academic support is being dealt with, and some suggested future directions.

The Librarians Association of the University of California (LAUC) appointed an Ad Hoc Committee on Library Instruction early in 1974. It was chaired by Beverly Toy, University of California, Irvine, and was charged with the responsibility to:

1. Compile information on existing library instruction programs on UC campuses.

2. Facilitate the exchange of instructional material and compile a collection of this material for distribution to nine campuses ... (This was never implemented, probably because of the existence of the California Clearinghouse on Library Instruction).

3. Prepare a report on significant gaps in library instruction programs.

4. Prepare a report for the information and possible action of the LAUC Assembly.

In the spring of 1976, the Final Report of the Ad Hoc Committee on Library and Bibliographic Instruction was submitted to the LAUC Assembly, together with a minority report.

Each of the campuses offers library instruction and the report describes these. The Berkeley campus has been offering a highly successful three-unit course entitled Bibliography I since the late 60's. It is always overenrolled; this fall 1,100 students preenrolled and 450 were assigned to classes. These classes were taught by three librarians who worked at Berkeley and seventeen librarians who did not. After some eight or nine years, there are not enough librarians at Berkeley available to teach even the forty percent of the students who wanted to take the course. Originally Bibliography I was offered as an experimental course but is now under the aegus of the School of Librarianship, which pays the salaries of the seventeen and reimburses the library for the three librarians at the rate of ten hours per week. The fact that only three librarians from a large staff are willing to teach is a point to ponder over.

UCLA, in addition to its self-paced course, which I will talk about later, offers a four-unit course entitled Information Resources and Libraries. This course is accredited by the Library School, which reimburses the library at the rate of ten hours per week for librarians who teach the course. The school intends to limit enrollment to four sections per quarter of twenty students each.

Berkeley and UCLA are the only campuses with library schools; the others have had to scramble for a departmental home. UC Davis librarians give a three-unit bibliography course in the English department and are designated "Lecturers in English." UC Santa Barbara and UC San Diego's courses are accredited in an interdisciplinary series. UC San Francisco librarians give a two-unit course out of the Department of the History of Health Sciences. UC Riverside and UC Santa Cruz give non-credit lectures and seminars. UC Irvine's Humanities Department sponsors a two-unit course given by librarians.

The report then goes on to note: "The interview and negotiations necessary to bring about the courses were not always pleasant. The qualifications of librarians to teach is always subtly (and sometimes not so subtly) questioned. The academic content of the courses is apt to be challenged, and the courses dismissed as remedial or skill courses. Curricular matters and the approval of courses are within the domain of the Academic Senate on each campus, and librarians are, by definition as non-Senate academic employees, excluded from the governing bodies. Gaining approval for the courses thus required negotiations with a club of which we are not members."

The final recommendations contained in the report are:

1. "That the University of California libraries be recognized as academic departments in their own right, responsible for initiating and conducting courses taught by librarians."

2. "That librarians teaching such courses use their own academic titles as librarians, Assistant Librarian, Associate Librarian, Librarian, and that these academic titles qualify them to serve as Officers of Instruction."

3. "That library budget formats be examined and revised to identify and provide for such courses, with the full-time equivalent of students taking library instruction courses becoming a component in the building of library budgets to generate positions based on such enrollment for the library."

"In brief, the Committee sees the two major obstacles to successful continuation of these programs as being lack of a firm academic home and lack of firm budgetary support and recognition. We urge joint action of all concerned librarians in these areas."

A minority report recommended that libraries should not "use their experts and expend their dwindling share of state funds to assume formal roles as teaching departments. . . Instead, we should encourage teaching departments on every campus to fulfill. . . their own teaching responsibilities so that all can be assured of the opportunity to become knowledgeable users through courses of instruction. . . (and) that courses in library instruction be recognized by the University Administration as essential to the curricula. . . and that at least one teaching department on each campus be required to sponsor such a class." These recommendations reflect the concerns of librarians everywhere and represent an approach being taken by a number of libraries.

Unfortunately most libraries have not been able to get the kind of support requested by these librarians at the University of California. However, even in cases where libraries are recognized as teaching departments, as with many community and junior college libraries, the institution is rarely willing or able to support traditional classroom courses in library instruction for more than a small percentage of the student body. The University of Minnesota has 8,000 entering students annually; Pennsylvania State University has 6,700. It is not even possible to give this number of students guided tours of the library, much less to give all of them classroom instruction.

An approach which many libraries have taken is the self-paced, self-directed library skills program. At least fifty academic libraries (and the number is doubtless a great deal higher) have taken this approach, most of them employing adaptations of the *Workbook in Library Skills* developed at UCLA. The program is designed to acquaint students with the facilities and resources of a given library, as well as to familiarize them with such basic reference tools as dictionaries, encyclopedias, atlases, almanacs, book reviewing and biographical sources, periodicals and news indexes and abstracts, etc. The basic workbook has twenty assignments but is looseleaf, so that assignments may be added or subtracted. The average time to complete the program is six hours. At most libraries, students purchase the book, complete it, and turn it in to the librarians without ever meeting in a classroom; it is totally a library approach. Librarians supervise the correction of the books by student assistants, and assign the grade (usually A or F, Pass or Fail). There is as much individual contact, as much one-to-one relating to the students as the librarians or the students want and/or have time for. Some librarians take the opportunity to discuss a reference tool when they hand it to a student, others arrange for interviews with all or some or a sampling of students when the workbooks are turned in; a variety of opportunities for interaction are possible. UCLA has prepared one hundred sets of question and answer sheets which can be adapted by any library; this means that in a class of one hundred, no two students will have the same set of questions. In a class of 6,700 students, there would be 67 students floating around with the same workbook, but their chances of finding each other are not good.

Students at many institutions are required to purchase the workbook and the proceeds from the sale cover the costs of printing the book, adapting UCLA's questions, writing new questions, replacing and rebinding of reference books, hiring additional reference desk assistance, and hiring students to correct the workbooks. The course in these cases is completely self-supporting, not costing the library or the institution anything. Some institutions have elected to absorb some or all of these costs.

In addition to making it economically feasible to offer library instruction to large numbers of students, the self-paced concept has been adapted for a number of other reasons:

1. The program is almost indefinitely expandable, not only because it can pay its own way but because it requires a much lower ratio of professional or teaching staff to students than traditional classroom courses. Even if there were funding to employ the dozens or hundreds of librarians which would be required to teach classes of several thousand, it would be virtually impossible to find them. In-house staff would soon be used up, as we have learned from the Berkeley experience, and finding sufficient numbers of outsiders familiar with the resources of a given library would be impossible in most cases.

2. The course complements guided orientation tours and individual library lectures on the one hand and advanced bibliography and library science courses on the other, since it lies somewhere between these, and therefore can, and should be offered in conjunction with already established tours and courses rather than as alternatives to them.

3. It can provide a minimal level of expertise in the use of the library on the part of all students in a class, which permits the instructor to make much more effective use of the library as a teaching tool. Thus an instructor can assign a literature search with the absolute assurance that every student in the class has had the experience of finding and successfully using three periodical indexes. Furthermore, every student has found books in the stacks, given the call number. Every student has found authors of books in the catalog, given the title; and titles of book, given the author. Every student has had the experience

of finding the subject of a given book in the catalog. Every student has found the answers to a set of questions in a score or more of basic reference tools. These students cannot necessarily give the authors, the titles or the publication history of a given set of encyclopedias, but they know where the encyclopedias are in their library and they have used several different sets of them. A common groundwork for research will thus have been established which every instructor can count on and build on.

4. Quite apart from its other advantages, actual experience with the program at UCLA, the University of Alaska, the University of Michigan, the University of Wisconsin, the University of Southern Colorado, the University of Washington and many others has elicited responses from the students who have taken the courses which have convinced the librarians involved with them that these courses represent a highly effective method of instruction in the use of the library. At UCLA, the Center for the Study of Evaluation included in a student questionnaire four questions relevant to Library Skills. The scores on the first two questions represent the mean distribution computed from the responses on a 1 low, 5 high continuum.

1. Extent to which Library Skills has been informative   4.59%

2. Extent to which it was helpful in other classes   4.29%

3. Should it be continued?   yes 94.00%

4. Comments: Helpful   15%
                Excellent   20%
                Should be required for all students   30%
                Should be required but taken less time   13%
                Should be offered but not required   8%

In conclusion, it is clear there is no one way to teach effective use of the library. We are in need of a variety and multiplicity of approaches. However, the economic facts of academic life as we know them today would seem to point to the self-paced library skills approach as the only viable method of reaching a significant proportion of the total college and university student population.

EMU's LIBRARY INSTRUCTION EXPERIENCES
IN THE 70's

Hannelore B. Rader
Orientation Librarian
Eastern Michigan University

Six years ago, at the First Annual Conference on Library Orientation for Academic Libraries held May 7, 1971 at Eastern Michigan University, participants heard a report of the new Library Outreach Orientation Program at EMU, which had been established with the help of joint financial support from the Council on Library Resources (CLR) and the National Endowment for the Humanities (NEH)*. This new program focused on course-related library instructhion to freshmen and sophomores in the humanities and social sciences.

We feel that it is appropriate at this Conference to present a progress report on the Library Outreach Orientation Program, particularly because the five-year grant terminated a year ago. Often when outside financial support terminates, a program may stop or change significantly. Also numerous librarians have expressed an interest to me in finding out what happened to the CLR-NEH supported library instruction programs after the grants stopped. It seems that the literature includes very little information on this. By the way, the final report of EMU's Library Outreach Orientation Program is available through the ERIC system, ED 115 265.

At last year's Conference we mentioned that EMU's Library Outreach Orientation Program was going to be continued. I would like to summarize the library orientation instruction activities for 1975-76, including various personal observations.

This year has been the most successful of the six years. A comparison of statistics (see below) shows that more library sessions were given to more students than in any of the previous years.

*Ann Andrew and Hannelore Rader, "Library Orientation is Reaching Out to People," *Library Orientation*, Papers presented at the Fifth Annual Conference on Library Orientation (Ann Arbor, Pierian Press, 1972), pp. 36-45.

Academic Year	Sessions given by Orientation	No. of Students	Sessions given by other Divs.	Total given in CER
1969-70	pre-program	–	141	141
1970-71	148	2,569	170	318
1971-72	124	2,930	164	288
1972-73	101	2,361	159	260
1973-74	142	2,801	174	316
1974-75	139	3,123	162	301
1975-76	158	3,185	179	337

Faculty involvement in and cooperation with the Library Orientation Program has also increased steadily. This again is demonstrated by the statistics showing that this year more library sessions were presented than previously. Some instructors in departments offering introductory undergraduate courses which include library work, who had previously not utilized the services of the Orientation Office, contacted the Orientation Librarian this year to plan cooperative library sessions. More instructors in the other departments cooperated with the Orientation Program. We are approaching the 100% participation goal in the freshman English composition and Speech courses. This is particularly noteworthy because of the changes in the instructional staff for English composition. In the past, these courses were taught predominantly by graduate teaching assistants and part-time instructors. The majority of these courses are now taught by full-time, tenured English professors who have not previously taught such courses and had therefore not participated in the Orientation Program. In view of this, their cooperation with the Orientation Librarian this year is exceptional as well as gratifying.

Our instructional materials for use in library sessions and as self-help are now at a level which we find acceptable on our campus. We have a total of seventy-four study guides on topics of interest to students. These guides are revised continually and displayed in the lobby of the University Library so that they are available whenever the building is open. We also have orientation materials available in this manner. There are printed sections on various services and a self-guided tour. The latter is also available in audio format. In addition we have an automated 20-minute slide-tape introduction to the Library stationed in the lobby. These materials are widely and continually publicized on campus and their use has increased steadily.

The staff of the Center of Educational Resources is supportive and cooperative in the area of library instruction. The Media Services staff is responsible for the creation of the audio visual materials and their smooth operation and so far we have never had a problem in this area.

The Library faculty in Public Services is involved in presenting library instruction to upper level and graduate courses. Objectives for library instruction have been adopted by the entire library faculty and have been publicized on campus. At present there is an elected Instruction and Services Committee within the Center of Educational Resources (CER) which deals with many issues including library instruction. The Orientation Librarian is an ex-officio member of this Committee.

The administration of the CER and the University have continued to be supportive of library instruction, recognizing that this is an integral part of library service to the University community. Their support has included encouraging librarians to obtain further education and to attend relevant professional activities.

Faculty and student support for the Orientation Program has also been documented. Questionnaires were sent to all faculty who participated in the Program. A summary of these questionnaires demonstrated strong support for the Program as seen in Appendix I.

Five hundred questionnaires were also sent to a random sample of senior students to determine if the Orientation Program has had an effect on students' knowledge of library skills and their attitude toward libraries and librarians. Unfortunately, only 22% of the students returned the questionnaires. Nevertheless, we felt encouraged by their responses, especially since we wanted to change their attitude toward librarians as part of the educational process. It seems that we are doing this through library instruction (see Appendix II).

During the five years of the Library Outreach Orientation Program, we surveyed thousands of students after the sessions to find out their reaction to these sessions. The majority indicated that they felt this was a very useful instructional service and that everyone should be required to have it.

Of course, much more testing in this area needs to take place and better and more scientifically designed testing instruments need to be used to assess the importance and impact of library instruction. The ACRL Task Force on Bibliographic Instruction is presently working on a research proposal in this area. All of us in library instruction are looking forward to the result of this study.

Another very interesting result of the Orientation Program and the increased library publicity on campus is an increase in reference and library use statistics in the last two years. In the early 70's we experienced a decrease in library use, but now this has changed. This year we noted a 20% increase in the use of library materials and in reference questions. It should be noted that the increase in reference questions is in the search category, not in the quick information type question. The latter has decreased. This, of course, means that reference librarians are increasingly busy with challenging reference questions and that reference and other library materials may have to be replaced more frequently because of heavy and continued use.

It is obvious that we think our orientation-instruction activities are successful. Let me tell you what has made them so. Library instruction is a lengthy and slow endeavor. It will not work if a program is in process for one or two years with few or no results and is abandoned. I feel a program should be tried for five or more years before real results can occur; after all, we are dealing with changing attitudes and that takes time. In our program, each year has been more successful. If you study other successful library instruction programs chances are they have been around more than five years (i.e. Earlham College).

Furthermore, a library instruction program needs to be flexible and related to the instructional needs of students and faculty. Also, since the campus population is a changing one and the library generally is not considered the most important service on campus, it is up to the library instruction staff to keep in constant communication with faculty and students. Continuous publicity and support from administration and the library staff are vital to the success of the library instruction program.

Perhaps this sounds like too much hard work and some of you will wonder if it is worth it. Library instruction is definitely hard work and if you are not willing to do it, it is best not to get into this type of library work. As to whether or not it is worth it, everyone will have to determine that individually. Library instruction is a challenge to the professional and offers an opportunity for creativeness and human service.

Eastern Michigan University
Center of Educational Resources
FACULTY EVALUATION
1970-1975

Total respondents:48
(of 99 solicited)
Response = 48%

During the past five years you have brought one or more classes to the Library for orientation sessions. We are very anxious to obtain evaluations of the Library Outreach Orientation Program from participating faculty members for inclusion in the final program report.

Please respond freely to each of the questions below and return the completed form to the Orientation Office, 217-H Library before the Winter Term ends. Please do *not* include your name.

Thank you for your cooperation,

Hannelore B. Rader, Orientation Librarian

1. Do you think your students are more confident in using the library having had a library session?
   YES (44)   NO (1)   COMMENT ONLY: (3)

   YES: 92% NO: 2%   COMMENT ONLY: 6%

2. Did your students produce papers showing evidence of a high(er) quality of documentation after having had the orientation session(s)?
   YES (35)   NO (6)   COMMENT ONLY: (7)

   YES: 73% NO: 13%   COMMENT ONLY: 14%

3. Are you now requiring more assignments which involve the use of the library?
   YES (22)   NO (21)   COMMENT ONLY: (5)

   YES: 46% NO: 44%   COMMENT ONLY: 10%

4. Will you continue to bring your students in for library instruction sessions?
YES (40)   NO (3)   COMMENT ONLY: (5)

YES: 83% NO: 6%   COMMENT ONLY: 10%

5. Has the Library Outreach Orientation Program helped you to become more aware of and more familiar with library resources?
YES (44)   NO (3)   COMMENT ONLY: (1)

YES: 92% NO: 6%   COMMENT ONLY: 2%

6. Should the Library Outreach Orientation Program be continued?
YES (47)   NO (0)   COMMENT ONLY: (1)

YES: 98% NO: 9%   COMMENT ONLY: 2%

7. How has your participation in the Orientation Program changed your attitude toward librarians as "contributors to student learning?"

No Response: (11) or 23%
Responses: (37) or 77%
  A. Indicating attitude change in positive direction: (6) or 16%
  B. Indicating reinforcement of positive attitude: (8) or 22%
  C. Indicating positive attitude without change: (13) or 35%
No one indicated negative attitude. (6) made other comments (or 16%).

SENIOR STUDENTS SURVEY
Data Summary

I. GENERAL INFORMATION ABOUT EVALUATORS
AT THE TIME OF THE SURVEY

Data:

AGE		SEX	
17--21	41%	Male	36%
22--30	48%	Female	61%
31--40	8%	NR	3%
40+	1%		
NR	2%		

RACE		CLASS STANDING	
American Indian	1%	Freshman	0
Chicano	1%	Sophomore	1%
Black	1%	Junior	1%
Caucasian	96%	Senior	95%
No Response	1%	Graduate	3%

GRADE POINT AVERAGE		EMU COLLEGE IN WHICH ENROLLED	
3.5--4.0	16%	Arts & Sciences	23%
3.0--3.49	41%	Education	47%
2.5--2.99	26%	Business	16%
2.0--2.49	12%	Applied Science	1%
Other	1%	Human service	1%
NR	4%	No Response	9%

BEGAN AT EMU AS FRESHMAN	
Yes	48%
No	52%

Art	2%	Home economics, Education	3%
Art, commercial	2%	Home economics, Family	3%
Biology	2%	Industrial Technology	1%
Business:		Library Science	1%
Accounting	8%	Math	1%
Education	2%	Music	1%
General	3%	Physical Education	1%
Management	1%	Phys. Ed. -- Recreation	2%
Marketing	3%	Political Science	3%
Secretarial	1%	Psychology	1%
Chemistry	2%	Speech & Dramatic Arts	15%
Computer Systems	3%	Special Eduation, gen.	9%
Dance	1%	Special Ed. -- Occupational	1%
Education, early el.	2%	Special Ed. -- Speech Path.	2%
Education, later el.	2%	Social Work	2%
English	4%	Social Science	1%
Geography, general	3%	No Response	7%
Geography, earth sci.	2%		
History	3%		
Home economics, gen.	2%		
Home economics, dietetics	2%		

II. LIBRARY ORIENTATION–INSTRUCTION EXPERIENCE (LOIE)

LOI Experience:
Key Question: Did you ever have a library orientation session, library tour, or library lecture presented by a librarian at EMU?
YES   54% (N=63) -- Hereon known as LOIs
NO   46% (N=53) -- Hereon known as NoLOIs

Number of LOI Experiences:
Those students who had library orientation--instruction experience(s) had their first session, tour, or lecture as follows:

Freshman year	44%
Junior year	21%
Senior year	21%
Sophomore year	10%
Graduate school	4%

35% of the LOIs had more than one orientation–instruction experience;
18% had three to five such experiences during their sophomore, junior, and/or senior year.

LOIE Departments and Classes:

	Those who had ONE session had it in: (N=41)	Those who had TWO sessions had them in: (N=11)	Those who had THREE sessions had them in: (N=6)	Those who had FOUR or FIVE sessions had them in: (N=5)
Education	27%	18%	33%	28%
English	29%	36%	17%	11%
Business	24%	18%	11%	5.5%
Geography	2%	4.5%		
Government			5.5%	
Math				5.5%
Library Sci	2%	4.5%	11%	28%
Poli Sci	2%	4.5%		
Speech	2%			5.5%
History				5.5%
Science				5.5%
Tour	7%	4.5%	17%	
Veterans			5.5%	
Can't remb.	5%	5%		5.5%

93

Deparments and Courses through which LOIE was provided:
(N sessions=101)

	%Ss		%Ss
Business Department	16%	Library Science Dept	9%
Communications		A.V. Science Dept	
Consumer Education		General Reference	
Investments 354		Library Orientation	
Personnel Admin.		Organiz of Materials	
Personnel Management		Selection & Use	
Personnel Problems			
Retailing		English Department	26%
Statistics 365		Children's Literature	
		English Comp. 121	
Education Department	27%	English Comp. 122	
Ed. Psychology		Journalism	
EDP Measurement			
EDP Research		Geography Department	2%
EDP Statistics		Field Geography	
Health Ed.		Research	
Health Ed. -- Elem.			
Industrial Ed.		Math Department	1%
Methods of Teaching:		Political Sci. Dept	1%
Biology		Science	1%
Math		Speech, Research in	1%
Reading		Veterans groups	1%
Science		Library Tour by Librarian	
Social Studies		Librarian	6%
Speech			
History Department	2%	Can't remember	6%

III. EVALUATION OF LOIE BY STUDENTS

Summary: Most of those students who had LOI (N=63) felt it was worth their time (89%) and that it prepared them, at least somewhat, for their library assignments (91%).

Data:

LOI was worth time:		LOI prepared them for library assignments:	
YES:	89%	A great deal:	32%
NO:	11%	Somewhat:	59%
		Not at all:	9%

IV. LOIs VERSUS NoLOIs

Library Usage:
    Key Question: Do you use libraries (EMU and others) a) regularly;
                  b) rarely; c) never?

Data: Observed frequencies of library use of 115 Ss
                         (percentages appear in brackets)

Ss	Regularly	Rarely	Never	TOTAL
LOIs:	40 (63%)	22 (35%)	1 (2%)	63
NoLOIs:	32 (52%)	19 (37%)	1 (2%)	52
*TOTAL	72 (63%)	41 (36%)	2 (1%)	115

*one student did not respond

Use of Basic Information Sources:
    Key Question: Have you used such information sources as:
                  a) New York Times; b) Monthly Catalog; c) Social
                  Sciences & Humanities Index; d) ERIC (Research
                  in Education)?

Data: Percent of LOIs (N=63) & NoLOIs (N=53) who
                    have used each of the four basic information
                    sources.

Ss	NYT	MC	SS&HI	ERIC
LOIs	49%	46%	60%	35%
NoLOIs	38%	42%	49%	19%

Observed frequency of use of each source by
LOIs and NoLOIs.

No. titles used	No. LOIs	No. NoLOIs
4	6	2
3	15	9
2	18	16
1	15	11
0	9	15
	N= 63	N=53
	$\Sigma X_1 = 120$	$\Sigma X_2 = 78$
	$\bar{X}_1 = 1.9$	$\bar{X}_2 = 1.5$

Use of Reference Sources in Subject Major:
　Key Question: A. Are you familirar with the major reference
　　　　　　　　sources in your subject major?
　　　　　　　B. If so, name as many titles as you can up to five.

　Data:　　A. Self reported familiarity with major's sources:

Observed frequencies of "familiarity" responses
of 114 Ss (percentages appear in brackets)

Ss	Familiarity			
	Very	Somewhat	Not at all	TOTAL
LOIs	24 (38%)	30 (48%)	8 (13%)	62
NoLOIs	16 (30%)	27 (51%)	9 (17%)	52
Total	40 (35%)	57 (50%)	17 (15%)	114

B. Observed frequency: acceptable titles named by
　53 NoLOIs and 63 LOIs.

Ss	Total Number of Acceptable Titles
LOIs	99 (71%)
NoLOIs	41 (29%)
TOTAL	140

No. Acceptable Titles Named	f LOIs	f NoLOIs
5	8	1
4	3	2
3	6	4
2	9	5
1	11	6
0	26	35
	N=63	N=53
	$\bar{X}$=1.57	$\bar{X}$=.77

Attitude Toward Libraries:

Key Question: How do you view libraries in general: a) as a source for all types of information; b) as a place to get help for class work; c) as a study place; d) as a place for social gathering; e) other?

Data: Observed frequencies of "view of Libraries" responses of 116 Ss (percentages in brackets)

Ss	All types information	Class--work help	Study	Social	Oth.	Total
LOIs	57 (50%)	21 (19%)	24 (21%)	2 (2%)	9 (8%)	113
NoLOIs	43 (49%)	19 (22%)	19 (22%)	4 (5%)	2 (2%)	87
Total	100 (86%)	40 (34%)	43 (37%)	6 (5%)	11 (9%)	200

Attitude Toward EMU Librarians:

Key Question: How do you view librarians at EMU? a) as instructors who help you use the library; b) as guardians of books; c) as information specialists; d) other.

Data: Observed frequencies of "view of EMU librari-- ans" responses of 116 Ss (63 LOIs, 53 NoLOIs). (percentages in brackets)

Ss	Instructors	Guardians	Info. Specs.	Other			TOTAL
				Pos.	Neut.	Neg.	
LOIs	39 (62%)	6 (10%)	20 (32%)	4 (6%)	1 (2%)	6 (10%)	76
NoLois	30 (57%)	12 (23%)	23 (43%)	3 (6%)	1 (2%)	4 (8%)	73
Total	69	18	43	7	2	10	149

EMU Library Confidence

Key Question: Do you generally feel confident in the EMU
Library (i.e. do you feel you can ask any type of
information question and you will receive an
adequate answer)?

Data: Observed frequencies of "EMU Library Confidence"
responses of 116 EMU senior students.

Ss	Unreluctant & Confident	Reluctant & Not Confident	Total
LOIs	56 (89%)	7 (11%)	63
NoLOIs	35 (66%)	18 (34%)	53
Total	89	24	113

OBJECTIVE TESTS AS AN EVALUATION TOOL: PROBLEMS IN CONSTRUCTION AND USE

Susan Burton
Reference Librarian
Undergraduate Library
University of Texas at Austin

At the Undergraduate Library at the University of Texas at Austin our initial experiences administering objective pre and post tests to experimental and control groups have taught us that evaluation doesn't necessarily provide answers, it may just raise more questions. Before discussing some of the problems associated with objective testing, I'd like to tell you something about the instructional program we have been evaluating.

During the past year we have developed and implemented a program of course-integrated instruction which is part of a required freshman English course. This semester we reached over 3,700 students in 150 sections. Even with three librarians devoting half time to instruction it would be impossible to meet individually with each of these classes; therefore, instruction is print-based and self-paced. It spans the entire semester of freshman English. The end product is a term paper. Students work through a series of library Study Guides and worksheets. The worksheets are designed to add items to students' working bibliographies. They are assigned at one or two week intervals in search strategy order.

The library's goal is for students to master the fundamentals associated with effective use of encyclopedias, the card catalog, and indexes. They are expected to be able to plan and carry out a basic search strategy. Although students aren't required to memorize specific titles, they should recognize that there are categories of reference materials which include both general and specialized sources.

Since ours is an entirely new program, we know that a period of development and modification will be necessary before these objectives can be fully realized. Consequently, we are trying to evaluate our instruction from as many angles as possible. This includes cost analysis, attitude surveys completed by students and instructors, analysis of bibliographies, compilation of reference and circulation statistics, and informal observations and conversations. If we were relying solely on the preceding types of evaluation, at this point our reference staff would be complacently resting on its laurels.

This is not to imply that these forms of evaluation didn't indicate the need for some modifications. However, we know we succeeded in familiarizing students with the library and with a variety of reference materials. Attitude surveys indicated students became more confident. Reference statistics for one month alone increased 83% over last year, so we know students are interacting more with librarians. Most important, we are positive students found the information necessary to write papers because we've reviewed representative bibliographies.

On the other hand, our experience with objective testing as a method of evaluation challenged assumptions we didn't know we had. Despite the outcome of other types of evaluation, the test results have led us to have doubts about how much students really learn from one successful library experience.

At this point a short summary of some of the advantages and drawbacks associated with objective tests is in order. Objective tests are attractive because, compared to practicums or subjective tests, they are easy to administer and easy to grade. The results are simply quantified and lend themselves either to pre and post instruction comparisons or comparisons between groups instructed by difference methods. Objective tests are particularly useful for identifying strengths or gaps in students' knowledge. Instruction can then be modified accordingly.

On the other hand, librarians find that there are definite limitations to what can be evaluated with an objective test. True and false, multiple choice, and identification test items can measure whether students recall specific facts and principles about library materials and procedures; however, they cannot measure changes in behavior or actual success in finding material. Recall and behavior in a real library situation are not always analogous. This implies that not all objectives of a library's instructional program are likely to lend themselves to evaluation by an objective test.

Another problem is test construction. Due to the paucity, quality, and inappropriateness of the tests currently available, most librarians find it necessary to construct their own. This is an extremely time-consuming process. Test items must be screened carefully to insure that they relate directly to program objectives. In other words, the test must have external validity. A test may be faultlessly constructed, but the results will be meaningless in terms of program evaluation if test items do not determine whether specific instructional goals have been met. Although this seems self-evident, the major criticism that can be leveled at most library skills tests is that they lack external validity.

The refinement of a testing instrument is a long, cumulative process. It takes time to construct questions, decide on distractors (reasonable incorrect alternatives), pilot the test, and validate and revise individual test items. Statistical computer programs are an asset in determining a test's internal validity. If the test has internal validity, the test items will accurately discriminate between good and poor students.

Although results from a carefully constructed objective test can indicate whether students recall desired facts, one can't really attribute scores to the impact of an instructional program unless control groups have also been tested. In designing a research project aimed at assessing the effect of course-integrated library instruction in freshman English, we have found it very difficult to find and maintain uncontaminated control groups. During the past year we have given pre and post library skills tests to experimental sections who received library instruction and wrote term papers and to control sections who did not. This sounds relatively straightforward, but comparisons of the test results we obtained have proven to be practically useless because of the many variables which may have skewed the scores. Among these variables are: the innate abilities of different groups, instructor attitudes and behavior, the amount of library work students are doing in other classes, the availability of reference and point-of-use instruction in the library, and behavior changes attributable to the effect of singling groups out (the Hawthorne effect).

Even though objective tests are easy to score, the analysis and interpretation of results are not simple procedures, particularly when pre/post and experimental/control comparisons are involved. We have received conflicting advice and interpretations from people from six different campus departments and agencies. Research design is clearly as much an art as a science! The preliminary results of this semester's pre and post objective tests show that both experimental and control sections improved significantly, though the experimental groups improved more. There were a number of test items that showed no improvement, and, on the whole, scores were lower than we had anticipated. In our efforts to explain these results, we have been considering factors which may have implications for other library instruction programs.

One factor we suspect may have influenced test results is that we were measuring long term retention. Most library skills tests with which I'm familiar measure short term retention since they are administered immediately following instruction. On the other hand, our test was essentially a final on material covered during a four month period. Moreover, it was a final for which students were neither asked nor expected to study. We wonder whether the results of a test measuring long term retention would be any different regardless of the method of instruction, whether it was a series of lectures, a self-paced workbook, individual consultations, or a separate course. We also wonder how students' responses on an evaluation tool are influenced by grades or the lack of grades. How would test scores be effected if a grade were attached and students were told to prepare for the test? If test scores were higher as a result, would this mean that the instructional program was more successful or simply that students were proficient at memorizing and regurgitating facts?

Reviewing our test and similar ones developed at other institutions, we wonder if librarians aren't making too many assumptions about the amount of factual knowledge people need in order to have successful library experiences. How important is it for a student to be able to label the elements in a *Readers' Guide* entry or arrange a series of call numbers in the correct order? As far as I know librarians haven't yet established the relationship between these paper and pencil exercises and the ability to find material on the shelf. We don't know enough about the way people use common sense, context, and visual clues to locate information. There is an explanation and key to abbreviations in the front of each index volume. The logic of call number arrangement can be deduced on location in the library stacks. Recall on a test and success in an actual library situation are thus not necessarily analogous. Can more accurate tests be constructed?

In summary, after an initial experience with objective pre and post testing of experimental and control groups, my colleagues and I feel we have more questions than answers. We are prepared to continue experimenting with objective tests in an effort to determine the effect of different variables. I encourage you to do the same. A particularly intriguing avenue for investigation is the relationship between objective tests and other types of evaluation. Many students who score poorly on an objective test turn in bibliographies which document their ability to find information appropriate to their needs. Conversely, bibliographies produced by some of the students with the highest scores can be disappointing. By the same token, students' attitudes toward the library and their subjective estimates of how much they have learned do not necessarily correlate with scores on an objective test. We need to have a better understanding of these relationships.

Librarians who do choose to administer objective tests should do so with the knowledge that they are evaluating only one aspect of their instruction, its impact on students' short term retention of facts and abstract procedures. Librarians should also recognize that the construction of a valid test is a laborious process. However, until the profession reaches a concensus regarding library instruction objectives and the specific details which are important for students to master, it is unlikely that a standardized test can be developed for use in lieu of tests constructed locally to evaluate particular programs. Despite their inherent limitations, objective tests are an important tool because they provide data that can only be inferred from other types of evaluation. They are practically guaranteed to make us face up to whatever assumptions we have about what students know, don't know, or should know about finding information in libraries.

LIBRARY USE STUDIES
and the
UNIVERSITY OF COLORADO EXPERIENCE

Susan Edwards
Economics Bibliographer
University of Colorado

Even a cursory search through the library literature will illustrate the impossibility of summarizing, in the few minutes alloted today, the work done on user studies; and when compacted into five minutes, much of what I say will sound predominately and, perhaps, totally negative. I wish to emphasize, therefore, that properly designed user studies can perform an important role in the developing and strengthening of library instruction programs. If done well, they can explain phenomena and test for cause and effect relationships. Also, although I think what we have done at the University of Colorado is typical of much of what is being done elsewhere, the practice of self-criticism has much to recommend it; so I shall use our surveys as examples of the problems encountered in the developing of user studies. In addition I shall address my remarks to studies designed for and done at particular institutions since it is with these that most of us will be involved. I feel, however, that the time and effort spent on these local and generally descriptive studies could be better used to develop more generalizable, explanatory studies in which large populations are sampled and hypotheses formulated and tested.

What then has been our experience? First it is important to emphasize that our difficulties have not been due primarily to technical considerations; by this I mean problems which arise from methodological questions such as item construction, statistical analysis, and sampling procedures. The major hurdles have been those where librarians and not statisticians must provide the framework.

The four problem areas I wish to identify are the questions of 1. what do we need or want to know? 2. What data or information will best answer this need? 3. How are we going to conceptualize the variables? and 4. what norms are appropriate when interpreting the results?

105

Let us first look at questions 1 and 2, what do we need or want to know? and what data or information will best answer this need? Though the importance of exploring these questions may be self-evident, the indepth analysis which they demand is often overlooked. For example, very early in the project it was decided that we would try to evaluate systematically the effects of the program. One of the outcomes to be measured was the changes in amount of library use in the two participating Departments -- Economics and History; therefore, we did define a need, at least in a rudimentary way. The next step was to determine what data would allow us to measure this change. Unfortunately it was at this stage that we failed to analyze the data requirements adequately, although it was obvious we would need measures of use at the beginning and end of the grant. To measure amount of use we surveyed all History and Economics students and a random sample of the remaining undergraduates. The results of the first survey show a significant difference in the amount of use by History students. Although this is interesting, what will we know when we survey again at the fifth year? I suspect not much for we did not find out why there were differences among the groups or what variables may be accounting for these differences. If at the end of the grant the amount of use by History and Economics students has decreased relative to other students, should we assume that the grant activities have led to this decreased use? Intuitively and, perhaps, logically we would respond "of course not" but this answer is going to hard to justify using the data we have collected to this date. There are so many alternative explanations: teaching methods or library activities external to the grant program may have changed non-participating students' behavior; or the socioeconomic characteristics of the students in the various departments may have changed. There is evidence that these socioeconomic factors may be important in determining use even in academic libraries. The important thing is that we could have tried to hold constant some of these variables if we had carefully analyzed what we needed to know to achieve our goals.

The third problem with user studies is the difficulty of conceptualizing the variables, or stated another way: what are the elements which constitute the phenomenon? In one of the surveys the students were asked how successful they were in locating "the right information," the concept here being "right information." If their responses were below a certain level, they were asked to indicate why they were unsuccessful; options such as "I could not find it in the catalog." or "the material was not on the shelf" were given. This is a good example of a very narrow defining and incomplete conceptualizing of the process of locating the "right information." A complete conceptualization would have questioned such factors

106

as whether the students were able to find material at the desired level of technical difficulty, of the appropriate currency, and from the desired point of view; for surely something on the shelf that is from an unappropriate frame of reference is no more help than the right material off the shelf.

The final issue I want to discuss is the importance of norm references. On one of the questionnaires we asked students how often they approached librarians for help; the results show that approximately 30 percent of the students normally seek assistance from a librarian. The question then becomes whether to report this as only 30 percent of the students ask for help, or to say that as many as 30 percent seek assistance. Without a comparison it is difficult to interpret the statistic. It might be interesting know how many students ask art dealers for help when choosing a print, or even if they ask a salesperson when they don't see a book on the bookstore shelf. This may seem a little far-fetched, but there may be general patterns which govern when people request assistance. Researchers in other fields have found behavioral patterns, and their findings may have some applicability to library research. For example in the 1940's Herbert Hyman found that people's ignorance about particular issues may not be a result of a lack of publicity about the issues but may be due to "a persistent habit of certain individuals to avoid exposure to knowledge."* Knowing the magnitude of this phenomenon might be helpful in knowing what maximum response to expect when offering library instruction programs.

This is a good lead into my final point which is how many problems could be avoided by beginning with a competent and thorough search of the literature. Every day in our professional lives we stress the importance of knowing and building on prior knowledge. Why then do so many user studies reflect ignorance of the hundreds of studies which have been done? There are many bibliographies of user studies; and, even more valuable, a number of competent reviews of the literature which show some questions already have been answered, some of the pitfalls to avoid, and what profitable areas we might explore. In these times, when certain groups such as students are being surveyed so extensively, to waste their goodwill and our time on studies which go into a file never to be referred to again does a disservice to everyone involved.

*Herbert Hyman and Paul B. Sheatsley. "Some Reasons Why Information Campaigns Fail." *Public Opinion Quarterly* 2 (Fall, 1947): 412-423.

EVALUATING FACULTY INVOLVEMENT
IN LIBRARY INSTRUCTION

Ben LaBue
History Bibliographer
University of Colorado

Last year at this conference Susan Edwards reported some of the more interesting findings from our survey of faculty on undergraduate library skills. Rather than discuss that specific project again I want to share with you some observations as an amateur about evaluation in general and evaluation of faculty in particular. I think the questions "so what" and "why bother" are crucial and need to be asked and answered before embarking on any evaluation effort. I am not advocating that evaluation be ignored where it is presently non-existent or abandoned where it already exists, but that any evaluation project be carefully thought out in terms of what is to be measured and what is to be done with the results.

A too common reaction to the results of evaluations seems to be "well, so what?" Unfortunately, as Ms. Edwards has indicated, perhaps this reaction has not been common enough. Information is being gathered, but what does it mean? This problem can be corrected if careful consideration is given during the planning stages to just what the information obtained will mean. Does a yes answer mean the respondent agrees with the question or disagrees with the negative response? What does it mean when a question is answered "sometimes" as opposed to "always?" It is not enough to devise mechanically correct questions and formats for answering the questions. Mechanically correct questions do not in any way guarantee useful information. We can and probably should get outside help when designing evaluation instruments, but we as librarians have the responsibility to insure the questions asked are really the ones we want answered.

The question "why bother?" should be asked when considering the various possible results of an evaluation project. For instance when evaluating a program of library instruction an obvious question is "What impact is the program having on the campus population?" I might add that this question is perhaps more obvious to budget administrators than to those doing library instruction. Unfortunately, at this stage of development, most programs of library instruction on most campuses seem to be reaching only a very small percentage of the student population. This in no way denies the value of such programs; it is simply a fact of life, one that most of us do not like to admit, however. Once it is admitted that the value of the program outweighs the impact of the program on the total population, the question, however obvious, becomes irrelevant. It may be an area of concern, but if the program is going to continue whether one or one hundred students are reached, then concentrate your evaluation effort on the contents of the program. In other words, if you are going to deny the importance of the information after it has been gathered or will not use it in the decision-making process, do not gather it in the first place. Which leads me into the question at hand – "Why evaluate the teaching faculty?"

The teaching faculty at best are only marginally involved in library instruction even in programs such as ours at the University of Colorado where we are trying to incorporate library instruction into the curriculum. The teaching faculty may be supporters, even enthusiastic supporters, it may be that library instruction cannot succeed without their support, but they are still only marginally involved in library instruction. It is our responsibility as librarians to design, develop, promote, conduct and evaluate library instruction. The deeper library instruction penetrates the maze of classroom and curriculum the less the need for evaluation of faculty. When library instruction is to be imparted through classroom participation, then the relevant faculty measure is the number of classrooms or courses with such arrangements, and this does not require an elaborate evaluation instrument.

What about faculty evaluation for programs of library instruction not using the course-integrated approach? I will answer the question with a question, "Why bother?" The burden for answering that question is on you. You must justify the effort, and be willing to modify your program if it is so indicated by the evaluation. If you cannot or will not, then do not do it.

We conducted a faculty survey at the University of Colorado; why did we bother? The questionnaire we developed, used and reported on last year was designed to establish a datum line from which we could measure changes in faculty attitudes. The information we gathered as a result of the questionnaire was not intended to stand alone though many questions and answers do; in a sense, it was a pre-test. Toward the end of our project we can repeat the survey to see if any changes in attitudes have occured. It is too early to say whether we will achieve our purpose, but I suspect that we will end up with the indications of change with no indication whether the changes are good or bad or even the results of the

the project. This is partially due to the design of the questionnaire, but I think more significantly, to changes that are occuring independently of the project. The College of Arts and Sciences just recently adopted a rule that all departments within the college will offer two writing courses each year. These courses are to emphasize writing and not research, but most certainly they will have some effect on the data we collect from now on. Would we do it again? Personally, I think we would. The program of library instruction that Ms. Edwards and I are involved in is made possible by a grant from the Council on Library Resources and the National Endowment for the Humanities. Because of this grant we are able to spend half our time working in subject departments outside of the library; a very expensive feature of our project. We owe it to ourselves, our faculties, our funding agents, and our fellow librarians to engage in as much evaluation as possible. Would I recommend faculty evaluation for everybody else? No.

As academic librarians either interested in or involved in bibliographic instruction we should be most concerned with improving the quality of our instruction and expanding our programs, and not with measuring or surveying the teaching faculty who, in the end, serve only as facilitators.

APPENDIX I

Thursday Group Discussion
Steps to Follow to Set up a Program

I. Study your environment

   a. Study your academic environment (course, requirements, programs)

   b. Make a profile of your students

   c. Make an assessment of your library (materials, personnel)

   d. Discuss tentative ideas with administrators (library and others)

   e. Discuss tentative ideas with faculty

   f. Assess interest of all these groups regarding a library instruction program

   g. Decide which type of program would be most practical and effective in your situation

   h. Discuss your ideas and proposed program with entire staff and all administrators before finalizing the plans.

II. Plan the Library Instruction Program

   a. Write objectives for the planned program utilizing faculty, staff, and administrative input

   b. State your personnel needs in specific terms and provide clear responsibilities for each one

   c. List possible instructional materials to be prepared

   d. Compose a tentative budget

   e. Plan for some type of evaluation of the program

Friday Group Discussion
How to Implement a Program

I. Publicize the program to

    a. the library staff

    b. the faculty

    c. the students

    d. all administrators

II. Prepare instructional materials to support your library instruction

    a. printed guides, orientation handouts, worksheets, bibliographies, evaluations

    b. media materials if needed – transparencies, posters, slides tapes, films, videotapes

III. Test your program on a limited portion of your population to make ramifications

IV. Implement your program fully

    a. Involve as many members of your staff as possible

    b. Keep detailed statistics

    c. Do some evaluation each year

    d. Write yearly objectives

    e. Continue to publicize the program

LIBRARY ORIENTATION AND INSTRUCTION – 1975*
An Annotated Review of the Literature

Hannelore B. Rader
Eastern Michigan University

Beam, Karen G. "Library Instruction: Teaching a Survival Skill," *Hoosier School Libraries,* 14 (April, 1975), pp. 18–19.

This short article discusses the importance of teaching students of all ages the skills to gain access to any type of information through one or more intermediate codes or keys. The importance of teaching only when a need for it exists and cooperation with the teachers are stressed.

Beeler, Richard J. *Evaluating Library Use Instruction,* Ann Arbor, Michigan: Pierian Press, 1975.

These are papers which were presented at the University of Denver Conference on the Evaluation of Library Instruction, December 13–14, 1973. Different attempts toward evaluating library instruction programs are commented upon and many of the problems inherent in these evaluation attempts are pointed out.

Bolner, Mary. *Planning and Developing a Library Orientation Program,* Ann Arbor, Michigan: Pierian Press, 1975.

These are the proceedings from the Third Annual Conference on Library Orientation for Academic Libraries held at Eastern Michigan University, May 3–4, 1973. The publication contains information on planning a program, developing faculty–librarian cooperation, the administrative set–up of an orientation program, instructional methodology and evaluation of orientation programs.

Browning, E.K. "Solve the Mystery of Reference: Use 'Calendar Clue'," *School Library Journal,* 22 (October, 1975), pp. 71–4.

This article discusses a game to teach reference skills to children in the elementary grades. All directions and rules as well as an evaluation of the game are included.

Bryson, JoAnn. "Library Orientation and Instruction in North Carolina Academic Libraries," *North Carolina Libraries,* Summer–Fall, 1975, pp. 19–23.

This is a summary of library orientation–instruction programs in North Carolina academic libraries based on a 1973 survey. Tables summarizing the findings from seventy–three academic libraries are appended.

Reprinted from Reference Services Review, v4n4, October/December 1976, pp.91–93.

Burton, Hilary D. "Techniques for Educating SDI Users," *Special Libraries,* 66 (May--June, 1975), pp. 252-5.

This is a description of techniques developed by the author to train potential users of the Selective Dissemination of Information (SDI) system implemented within the U.S. Department of Agriculture. Through this training program for SDI users, the SDI service has been increased and such trained users may apply their newly--gained knowledge to other computer searching.

Cameron, Samuel H. And Messinger, Karlyn W. "Face the Faculty: Prevalent Attitudes Regarding Librarian--Faculty Relationship," *Pennsylvania Library Association Bulletin,* 30 (March, 1975), pp. 23--26 and 30 (May, 1975), pp. 48--51.

This is a two part summary of a presentation made at the Tri--State College Library Cooperative Annual Program Meeting, February 6, 1974. It discusses some of the causes of the conflict between faculty and academic librarians in regard to faculty status for librarians and librarians as instructors for library resources. Some remedies are suggested.

Condit, Martha O. "If only the Teacher Had Stayed With the Class," *Elementary English,* 52 (May, 1975), pp. 664--666.

This is a discussion of a library skills program for elementary English students and the importance of teacher--librarian cooperation.

Cook, Margaret G. *The New Library Key,* New York: Wilson, 1975.

This third edition updates the book and is again intended to be used as a textbook in library use courses, as supplementary reading in research methods courses and self--study manual for individual library users. The book includes chapters on various reference sources and research materials as well as a chapter on "writing a research paper." Also provided are appendices listing additional research materials for library users and instructional librarians.

Corlett, Donna. "Library Skills, Study Habits and Attitudes, and Sex as Related to Academic Achievement," *Educational and Psychological Measurement,* 34 (Winter, 1974), pp. 967--969.

This study investigated the relationship of library skills, study habits and attitudes, and sex to the academic achievement of college freshmen. The Library Orientation Test (Columbia, 1955) appeared to be a valid instrument for forecasting college success.

Dillon, Howard W. "Organizing the Academic Library for Instruction," *Journal of Academic Librarianship,* 1 (September, 1975), pp. 407.

Due to more professionalism among Sangamon State University librarians, library faculty can participate more closely in academic instructional activities by cooperating with the teaching faculty and through library instruction programs. Evaluations of the Sangamon program have indicated that it is successful. A job description for an instructional services librarian in appended.

Downs, R.B. and Keller, C.D. *How to do Library Research* 2nd ed., Urbana, Illinois: University of Illinois, 1975.
This is a new edition of the 1966 publication on library research for scholars and college students. Some general information about libraries, librarians and the nature of reference books are provided. Could be used as a textbook for a bibliography course.

Dyson, Allan J. "Organizing Undergraduate Library Instruction: The English and American Experience," *Journal in Academic Librarianship,* 1 (March, 1975), pp. 9--13.
The author reports on his Council on Library Resources--supported study of the administrative organization of library instruction programs for undergraduates in the U.S. and Great Britain. He investigated speci-- fically library instruction programs which utilized specific "library in-- struction librarians." His conclusion lists four specific patterns of library instruction programs.

Elza, Betty and Maslar, Isobel. "Refecol," *Science Teacher,* 42 (Novem-- ber, 1975), pp. 31–32.
This is a description of a project to encourage tenth grade students in language arts or science to learn about reference materials by utilizing their interest in ecology. The project is in the form of a game and rules and descriptions are included.

Essary, Kathy and Parker, Steve. "Educating your patrons," *Arkansas Libraries,* 32 (1975), pp. 16--29.
This article describes briefly the experience of academic librarians who prepared their first library orientation program in slide--tape format.

Frick, Elizabeth. "Information Structure and Bibliographic Instruction," *Journal of Academic Librarianship,* 1 (September, 1975), pp. 12--14.
The author attempts to describe the important role bibliographic instruction at the undergraduate level can play in educating the student. She suggests that information structure can be linked with library in-- struction methodology. Four levels of bibliography awareness are listed and described.

Hammond, Nancy. "Teaching Library Use," Cowley, John. *Libraries in Higher Education: the User Approach to Service,* London: Clive Bingley, 1975, pp. 83--101.
This chapter discusses problems inherent in library instruction in British Polytechnic institutions and two approaches to reader instruc-- tion – the tutor librarian and the subject specialist librarian. The author points out vital areas related to effective reader instruction such as

117

relations with faculty, methodology of the instruction, training of teaching librarians and teaching aids.

Hernon, Peter. "Library Lectures and Their Evaluation: A Survey,"
Journal of Academic Librarianship, 1 (July, 1975), pp. 14--18.
The author summarizes a survey of academic libraries, lectures to
classes and the role they play in library outreach programs. He documents
the various ways in which such lectures to classes are evaluated by the
librarians and offers suggestions for the future.

Hinchcliff, W.E. "RISE (Reform of Intermediate and Secondary Education) [and shine]," *California Librarian,* 36 (July, 1975), pp. 46--55.
This article proposes an experimental filmed course on media library
dynamics as a first step toward better, relevant and creative education.
The article further states that certain library skills should be a require-
ment for high school graduation. A bibliography on educational reform is
appended.

Lamprecht, Sandra J. "The University Library Map Room Orientation,"
Geography Map Division Bulletin, 98 (December, 1974), pp. 31--33.
This is a description of a 50–70 minute program to instruct students in
the use of a map library. Emphasis is on geographical reference materials.

Lolley, John L. "Educating the Library User," *Texas Library Journal,*
51 (Spring, 1975), pp. 30--32.
In this article the author discusses the evolution of an individualized
library instruction program at Tarrant County Junior College (Texas)
from a slide--tape--workbook program to a text--workbook approach.
Also discussed are the use of pre--and post--tests and the results of this
individualized library instruction.

Miller, Rosalind. "Why I Can't Create a Learning Center," *School Media
Quarterly,* 3 (Spring, 1975), pp. 215–218.
This article lists reasons which make it difficult to make the learning
center the central part of any school. The library media specialist at
Drew Elementary School in Atlanta, Georgia overcame many of the
listed reasons and worked closely with children K–7 from the inner city
with low reading and communication skills to interest them in learning.
Many of the activities she used are described.

Morse, G.W. *Concise Guide to Library Research.* 2nd rev. ed. New York:
Fleet Academic Editions, Inc., 1975.
This is a revised edition of the 1966 publication by the author. The
book is divided into three areas: key to research, key to reference books
and key to periodicals. The guide is intended for college students and
could be used as text for a bibliographic course. Subject and title indexes
are provided.

Nettlefold, Brian A. "A Course in Communication and Information Retrieval for Undergraduate Biologists," *Journal of Biological Education,* 9 (October, 1975), pp. 201–205.

This article describes how the Paisley College of Technology in Penn--sylvania is teaching their undergraduate biology students communication and information retrieval. The library staff is teaching a compulsory course in this area which covers the structure of scientific literature, foreign language terminology and the information network in the life sciences.

Penland, Patrick. "Library Use Instruction," *Encyclopedia of Library and Information Science,* New York: Marcel Dekkar, Inc., 1975, vol. 16, pp. 113--147.

This article summarizes library use instruction writings and activities and suggests future implications for effective information retrieval and improved librarian--client communicaiton.

Penney, Barbara. "Planning Library Instruction," Cowley, John. *Libraries in Higher Education: the User Approach to Service,* London: Clive Bingley, 1975, pp. 137--149.

The author discusses the subject specialist librarian's role in library instruction in Great Britain. She stressses the importance of good planning in cooperation with faculty. Various types of instruction are commented upon and how to plan the correct type of instruction for various types of students is summarized. The chapter ends with some comments on the value of library instruction.

Rabkin, Frieda H. *Learning Center Guide: Helene Fuld School of Nursing,* New York: 1975, 8p. ED 107233.

This is a printed guide to the Learning Center of the Helene Fuld School of Nursing with explanations of classification, the card catalog, reference books, etc.

Rader, Hannelore B. *Academic Library Instruction. Objectives, Programs, and Faculty Involvement,* Ann Arbor, Michigan: Pierian Press, 1975.

These are the papers presented at the Fourth Annual Conference of Library Orientation for Academic Libraries held at Eastern Michigan University, May 9--11, 1974. Included is information on various library instruction programs, library instruction for disadvantaged students and philosophical statements on the library's role in education.

Rawles, Beverly. *Group Library Tours for Disadvantaged Adults. Public Library Training Institutes Library Service Guide No. 13,* Morehead State University, Kentucky, Appalachian Adult Education Center, 1975, 20p. ED 108651.

This report suggests library tours for adult basic education classes and other disadvantaged adult groups. Guidelines and rationale for such tours are given. Supporting activities and materials are also suggested.

A list of pitfalls to avoid is included.

"Reader Education -- Two Comments," *Australian Academic and Re--search Libraries,* 6 (June, 1975), pp. 92–94.

Two lengthy comments on the "Draft Standards of Reader Education" [*Australian Academic and Research Libraries,* 4 (December, 1975)] are offered here. Some of the problems in this area are pointed out and the difficulty of applying such guidelines universally are discussed.

"Reader Services," Thompson, Sara K. *Learning Resources Centers in Community Colleges,* Chicago: American Library Association, 1975, pp. 101–105.

The author provides a brief summary of library instruction activities in community colleges based on her study of twenty--seven such campuses and their learning resource centers.

Reynolds, Catherine J. "Discovering the Government Documents Col--lection in Libraires," *RQ,* 14 (Spring, 1975), pp. 228--231.

The author discusses various methods to promote the use of the gov--ernment documents collection such as exhibits, handouts, publicity in the news media and instruction. The instruction can be course--related, self--paced, in the form of mini--workshops, in--service training for staff and outside librarians.

Rominger, Carol A. *Handbook for English 48; Introduction to Library Research and Bibliography,* Davis, CA. Univ. Library, 1975. 121p. ED 106 670.

This handbook is used for a course on library research which includes a term project, practical assignment and lectures on reference works, card catalog, serials research strategies, etc. Student objectives are spec--ified.

Ruthstein, Joel S. and Hacker, Betty. *Using the Morgan Library; a Tour and Exercise,* Ft. Collins, Colorado: Colorado State University, 1975, 20p. ED 107265.

Self guided exercises are used to orient students to the physical layout of the library and to teach them the use of basic reference tools and methods of library research.

Sadow, Sandra and Beede, Benjamin. "Library Instruction in American Law Schools," *Law Library Journal,* 68 (1975), pp. 17--32.

The articles summarizes library instruction in American law schools and compares these findings with library instruction in other academic settings. It was concluded that improvements in the currently--used library instruction methods in law schools are needed. Appended is a summary of survey questionnaires.

Schwarz, P.J. "Learning to Use Microform Equipment: A self Instruc--

tional Approach," *Microform Review,* 4 (October, 1975), pp. 262–5.

The author discusses a procedure for developing and utilizing self–instructional booklets as a means of helping users of microform. Several steps should be followed when writing such a guide from objectives and graphic presentation to testing.

"A Sequence of Library Skills," *Hoosier School Libraries,* 14 (February, 1975), pp. 18–20.

Provided here is a K–8 library skills program based on children's actual need. The entire suggested program is built into the classroom activities and promotes the idea of children helping each other.

Shannon, Michael Owen. *To Trace a Law: Use of Library Materials in a Classroom Exercise,* New York: City University of New York, 1975, 9p. ED 111431.

This exercise guides the students through the legislative process of a bill becoming a law. Students can select a topic of interest to search and pertinent reference works are linked to help them find background in–formation and Congressional information.

Shelton, John L. "Project Uplift: Cultivating the Library Habit," *Wilson Library Bulletin,* 50 (September, 1975), pp. 59–62.

This article describes an experiment in library orientation during 1974–75 when 600 fifth and sixth graders from 9 rural counties in Georgia participated in Project Uplift. This library orientation program sponsored by the public library in cooperation with the schools involved teaching the use of the card catalog, encyclopedias, the *Readers' Guide* to these students and helped develop favorable attitudes toward using public libraries.

Simmons, Robert M. *A Library User's Guide to ERIC,* Stanford: Stanford University, 1975, 34p. ED 107311.

This is a concise guide to the use of ERIC and instructions are provided for a sample topic search through the ERIC system.

Simon, Dorothy B. "A More Human Approach to Instruction in the Use of Academic Libraries," Josey, E. J. *New Dimensions for Academic Library Service,* Metuchen, N. J. : Scarecrow Press, Inc., 1975, pp. 169–174.

Several questions facing the instructional librarian are raised and various reasons for use instruction in academic libraries are provided based on the contemporary students. The author maintains that the success of library instruction depends on the human approach to it, using an effec–tive instructional method in each situation.

"Sixth–Form Library Visits," *Library Association Record,* 77 (April, 1975), pp. 79–81.

The article describes a user instruction program at the University of Sussex Library for sixth--form students. The university library staff offered this instructional program to them in preparation for their en--trance to a university. Utilizing fifteen assignments and working in groups of twenty to thirty, they introduced the students to a wide--range of library resources.

Stevenson, M.B. "Library Instruction and the Development of the Individual -- a Comment," *Journal of Librarianship,* 7 (January, 1975), pp. 66--68.
This is a comment on P. J. Hills' article published in the above journal in October, 1974. Stevenson criticizes Hills' comments for being too theoretical and feels that a more practical approach is needed particularly in the area of methods for user education. Stevenson also offers some critical thoughts on the use of media in library instruction. He urges that some thought should be given to objective evaluation of any user instruction program.

Smith, Gary M. "Library--Based Information Services in Higher Edu--cation: Towards a Reappraisal," *Aslib Proceedings,* 27 (June, 1975), pp. 239--246.
This is a critical appraisal of library information services offered in British academic libraries. The author suggests a carefully--planned service which includes all types of reference services and library instruction.

Thompson, M. "An AV Look at Library Skills," *Instructor,* 84 (January, 1975), pp. 110 and 112.
This short article presents a script for a slide--tape presentation on biographical materials to be produced by upper elementary students.

Ting, Robert N. "Library Workshops for Engineers, The Buffalo Experi--ment," *Special Libraries,* 66 (March, 1975), pp. 140--2.
The article discusses a series of workshops in the use of library re--sources held at SUNY Buffalo for practicing engineers. Helpful hints are supplied for anyone wishing to hold similar workshops.

Tietjen, Mildred C. "Library Instruction Improvement Association," *The Library Scene,* 4 (June, 1975), pp. 12--13.
The author provides a realistic assessment of library instruction and related problems in the academic setting affecting such instruction.

"Toward Guidelines for Bibliographic Instruction in Academic Libraries," *College and Research Libraries News,* 36 (May, 1975), pp. 137--139+.
These guidelines for bibliographic instruction in academic libraries were proposed by the ACRL Bibliographic Instruction Task Force.

Whitten, B. "Social Sciences Bibliography Course: A Client--Oriented

Approach," *Journal of Education for Librarianship*, 16 (Summer, 1975), pp. 25--32.

The article describes an experimental method to teach the social sciences bibliography course to library science students at the University of Southern California. The students worked with social sciences profes--sors and researchers to compile bibliographies for their actual research projects. Consultations between students and faculty members preceded the bibliographic work. Faculty members evaluated the final projects. Students felt this experience was very beneficial for their future library work and faculty gained new positive attitudes toward librarianship.

Eastern Michigan University
Sixth Annual Conference on
Library Orientation for Academic Libraries
May 13-14, 1976

PARTICIPANTS

Albright, Jane A.
Carson-Newman Coll.
Jefferson City, TN
37760

Allen, Sandra L.
Univ. of Minnesota
Minneapolis, MN
55455

Aluri, Rao
Univ. of Nebraska
Omaha, NE 68101

Baker, Jean S.
Siena Heights Coll.
Adrian, MI 49221

Baldwin, Julia
Univ. of Toledo
Toledo, OH 43606

Baugh, Joanne D.
Pennsylvania St. Univ.
Uniontown, PA
15401

Beaubien, Anne K.
Univ. of Michigan
Ann Arbor, MI
48109

Benson, Stanley H.
Oklahoma Baptist Univ.
Shawnee, OK 74801

BeQuette V. Louise
Salem College
Salem WV 26426

Berg, Peter
Adrian College
Adrian, MI 49221

Bessler, Joanne
Purdue Univ.
West Lafayette, IN
47906

Bouton, Marla
Kearney State College
Kearney, NE 68847

Braun, Carl F.
Xavier Univ.
Cincinnati, OH
45207

Browson, Charles W.
Christopher Newport
College
Newport News, VA
23606

Cain, Melissa
Univ. of Illinois
Urbana, IL 61801

Cammack, Floyd
Leeward Comm. College
Pearl City, Hawaii 96782

Carroll, Hardy
Western Michigan
Univ.
Kalamazoo, MI
49008

Centing, Richard R
Ohio State Univ.
Columbus, OH
43210

Chaffin, John
NE Oklahoma
State Univ.
Tahlequah, OK
74464

Ciliberti, Anne
Wm. Paterson Coll.
Wayne, NJ 07470

Clarke, Ann
SUNY at Buffalo
Buffalo, NY 14214

Collier, Bonnie
Yale Univ.
New Haven, CT
06520

Collins, Tom
Kearney State
College
Kearney, NE
66847

Cooper, David L.
Anderson College
Anderson, IN 46011

Coughlin, June M.
BGSU Firelands Camp
Huron, OH 44839

Crawford, Joyce E.
Trident Tech. College
North Charleston, SC
29405

Crosby, Corryn
Univ. of Nevada
Las Vegas, NV 89154

Culp, Diane
Univ. of Michigan
Dearborn, MI 48128

Damien, Yvonne M.
Loyola Univ.
Chicago, IL 60660

Denton, Ann
Memphis State Univ.
Columbus, OH 43210

Devlin, Patricia B.
Ohio State Univ.
Columbus, OH 43210

Downing, Joan K.
Idaho State Univ.
Pocatello, ID 83201

Dusenbury, Carolyn
Univ. of Utah
Salt Lake City, UT
84102

Ellis, Virginia R.
Miami Univ. –
Middletown
Middletown, OH 45042

Epps, Donna E.
Oberlin College
Oberlin, OH 44074

Espo, Harold L.
Earlham College
Richmond, IN 47374

Fennessy, Kathryn K.
Alfred Univ.
Alfred, NY 14802

Ferriero, David S.
MIT Libraries
Cambridge, MA 02139

Fischler, Barbara B.
Indiana Univ. –
Purdue
Indianapolis, IN
49202

Flandreau, Arthur
Berea College
Berea, KY 40403

Fleeger, Dale
Anderson College
Anderson, IN 46011

Fought, Joanne
Illinois Central Coll
East Peoria, IL 61635

Fowler, Jane E.
Bates College
Lewiston, ME 04210

Fox, Barbara S.
Madison College
Harrisonburg, VA
22801

Freeman, Michael Stuart
Dartmouth College
Hanover, NH 03755

Gadsen, Alice H.
Stanford Univ.
Stanford, CA
94305

Gardner, Ronald A
Adrian College
Adrian, MI 49221

George, Mary W.
Univ. of Michigan
Ann Arbor, MI
48109

Ghent, Gretchen
Univ. of Calgary
Calgary, Alberta
Canada T2N 1N4

Golden, Gary
Southern Illinois
Univ.
Carbondale, IL
62901

Golden, Virginia B.
Erie Comm. Coll.
South
Orchard Park, NY
14217

Gowdy, Laura E.
Illinois State
University
Normal, IL 61761

Greenwood, Larry
Univ. of Kentucky
Lexington, KY
40506

Gregory, Marion M
Oakland Comm.
College
Auburn Heights,
MI 48057

126

Gregory, Patricia
Radford College
Radford, VA 24142

Grimes, Janet G.
Russell Sage Coll.
Albany, NY 12108

Grossman, Mary Beth
USC Sch. of Dentistry
Los Angeles, CA 90007

Hall, Blaine H.
Brighan Young Univ.
Provo, UT 84602

Hamilton, Judity
Univ. of Wisconsin –
Parkside
Kenosha, WI 53140

Hardesty, Larry
DePauw Univ.
Greencastle, IN 46135

Heath, Fred
Radford College
Radford, VA 24142

Hitt, Charles
Mankato State Coll.
Mandato, MN

Hogan, Fannie B.
Clark College
Atlanta, GA 30311

Hogan, Sharon Anne
Univ. of Michigan
Ann Arbor, MI
48109

Holmes, Elizabeth A.
St. Andrews Presby-
terian Coll.
Laurinburg, NC 28352

Hubble, Gerald B.
Rockhurst College
Kansas City, MO 64110

Jones, Eva
Harvard University
Cambridge, MD 02139

Johnson, George T.
Central State Univ.
Wilberforce, OH 45384

Johnson, Peter A.
Stanford Univ.
Stanford, CA 94305

Johnston, Marjory
Cast Western Reserve
University
Cleveland, OH 44106

Joyce, Beverly A.
Univ. of Oklahoma
Norman, OK 73069

Judd, Blanche
SUNY at Oswego
Oswego, NY 13126

Kelto, Kathy R.
Univ. of Dayton Lib.
Dayton, OH 45469

Kennedy, Sister
Marie M.
Barry College
Miami Shores, FL 33161

King, Judith D.
Grand Valley St. Coll.
Allendale, MI 49401

King, S. Edna
Slippery Rock St. Coll.
Slippery Rock, PA
16057

Kirsch, Debbie
Russell Sage Coll.
Albany, NY 12206

Koren, Stefania
Manhattanville
College
Purchase, NY
10577

Lam, R. Errol
Bowling Green
State Univ.
Bowling Green,
OH 43403

Larson, Julie
Univ. of Wisconsin
Milwaukee, WI
53201

Lichtenberg, Rita
Indiana Univ.
Bloomington, IN
47401

Lincoln, John R.
Lansing Commu-
nity College
Lansing, MI 48914

Little, Cecily
Johns
Central Michigan
University
Mt. Pleasant, MI
48858

Mahon, Sister
Mary Noreen
St. Xavier College
Chicago, IL 60655

Manley, Nancy
Univ. of Illinois
Urbana, IL 61801

Maughan, Laurel
Oregon State Univ.
Corvallis, OR 97331

McCutcheon, Hazel J.
Pennsylvania State
University
Ogontz Campus
Abington, PA 19001

McGrew, Mary Lou
Univ. of Northern
Iowa
Cedar Falls, IA 50613

Melling, Ruth H.
Indiana Univ. -- Purdue
Fort Wayne, IN 46805

Mertins, Barbara
West Virginia Univ.
Morgantown, WV
26505

Nikkola, Beth
Stephen F. Austin
State Univ.
Nacogdoches, TX
75961

Moe, Claudia
West Virginia Univ.
Morgantown, WV
26506

Moushey, Janet
Erie Community
College – N.
Orchard Park, NY
14217

Nelson, Margaret
Ball State Univ.
Muncie, IN 47303

Newman, Lillian

Agnes Scott College
Decatur, GA 30030

Olson, John
Schoolcraft College
Livonia, MI 48151

Ormondroyd, Joan
Cornell Univ.
Ithaca, NY 14853

Papazian, Barbara L.
Michigan State Univ.
East Lansing, MI 48824

Pask, Judith M.
Purdue Univ.
West Lafayette, IN
47907

Perdue, Robert W.
Univ. of West Florida
Pensacola, FL 32504

Platou, Mary Jane
SUNY – Buffalo
Buffalo, NY 14215

Pontius, Jack E.
Pennsylvania St. Univ.
University Park, PA
16802

Powell, Antoinette P.
Univ. of Kentucky
Lexington, KY 40506

Powers, Kathleen A.
Boston College
Chestnut Hill, MA 02167

Renford, Beverly L.
Pennsylvania St. Univ.
State College, PA 16801

Ridgeway, Patricia M.

Winthrop College
Rock Hill, SC 29733

Rigg, Sarah L.
West Georgia Coll.
Carrollton, GA
30117

Roberts, Anne
SUNY – Albany
Albany, NY 12203

Robertson, Susan
Univ. of Maine
Orono, ME 04473

Robinson, Doris
Russell Sage Coll.
Albany, NY 12208

Rottsolk, Katherine
St. Olaf College
Northfield, MN
55057

Ruskell, Virginia
West Georgia Coll.
Carrollton, GA
30117

Sajdak, Bruce T.
Univ. of Houston
Victoria, TX 77901

Scherger, Mary E.
Indiana Univ.
Kokomo, IN 46901

Schott, Pamela
Hartford Community College
Bel Air, MD 21014

Schwass, Earl R.
Naval War College
Newport, RI 02840

Sharplin, C. David
Univ. of Alberta
Edmonton, Alberta
Canada T6G 0M1

Sherrill, Rebecca L.
Miami University
Hamilton, OH 45011

Shill, Harold B.
West Virginia Univ.
Morgantown, WV
26506

Shockley, Doris T.
Clark College
Atlanta, GA 30311

Skelton, Dortha
College of William
& Mary
Williamsburg, VA
23185

Snead, Ernestine
Michigan State Univ.
East Lansing, MI
48824

Stahl, Wilson M.
Stockton State College
Pomona, NJ 08240

Stanley, Shirley
Univ. of Minnesota
Minneapolis, MN
55455

Steele, Ruth A.
Pennsylvania St. Univ.
Monaca, PA 15061

Stewart, Barbara
Ball State Univ.
Muncie, IN 47303

Stoffle, Carla J.
Univ. of Wisc. –
Parkside
Kenosha, Wi 53140

Strahler, Clytie E.
Wittenburg Univ.
Springfield, OH 45501

Taylor, Joe K.
Virginia Polytechnic
Inst.
Blacksburg, VA 24060

Templeton, Mary Ellen
Duke Univ.
Durham, NC 27706

Thomas, Elizabeth H.
Pennsylvania St. Univ.
Mont Alto, PA 17237

Thompson, Gary B.
Ohio Northern Univ.
Ada, OH 45810

Tiefel, Virginia
Hiram College
Hiram, OH 44234

Tolman, James R.
Weber State College
Ogden, UT 84403

Tongate, John
Sangamon St. Univ.
Springfield, IL 62708

Treadway, Cleo
Tusculum College
Greenville, TN 37743

VanEss, James E.
Carroll College
Waukesha, WI 53186

Winkemulder, Don
Kellogg Community
Collete
Battle Creek, MI 49017

Violette, Judith L.
Indiana Univ. –
Purdue
Fort Wayne, IN
46805

Walker, Mary Edith
Memphis State
University
Memphis, TN
38152

Ward, James E.
David Lipscomb
College
Nashville, TN
37203

Weber, Mark
University of
Evansville
Evansville, IN
47714

Weddle, Karen S.
University of
Oklahoma
Norman, OK
73069

White, Mrs.
Exir B. University
Tuscaloosa, AL
35401

Williams, Maudine B
Ferron School of
Art, IUPUI
Indianapolis, IN
46202

Williams, Tim
Radford College
Radford, VA
24142

Williamson, Rosalie
Piedmont Virginia
Comm. College
Charlottesville, VA
22901

Wortman, William A.
Miami Univ.
Oxford, OH 45056

Yee, Sandra
Muskegon Comm.
College
Muskegon, MI 49443